Heather Cook
Vice President, Asia Pacific at Seism
(Sydney)
www.linkedin.com/in/2heather-cook

When Gunnar and I started working together, I was very excited and eager to pick his brain and steal some of his tips and tricks. This instantly took my Social Selling to the next level.

His thirst for knowledge, expertise, experience, and passion around this subject really shines through in every engagement. He is extremely collaborative and is open to sharing knowledge, connections or just a laugh with all. He loves to help level up others around him and also around the world.

Gunnar leads by example and practices what he preaches, consistently. Having a strategy, building and nurturing relationships, adding value and delivering on his commitments and goals. Would you like to take your Social Selling to the next level?

Cian McLoughlin
Founder & CEO of Trinity Perspectives, SaaS Start-up founder,
keynote speaker, author of "Rebirth of the Salesman" (Sydney)
www.linkedin.com/in/cianmcloughlin

Gunnar Habitz is one of those rare individuals who truly embraces the *social* in Social Selling.

His generosity of spirit, curiosity and thirst for knowledge ensures that not only does he seek out new ideas, but proactively shares these lessons with his network.

It comes as no surprise therefore that *Connect & Act – Systematic Social Selling* expands on this theme, weaving Gunnar's personal experience and research with long form interviews and shorter content segments, to deliver a very impactful and important new book.

Brad Wochomurka

Vice President, Global Partnerships at Hootsuite
(Indianapolis)

www.linkedin.com/in/brad-wochomurka

There are moments in life when you get to witness the intersection of passion and knowledge for certain individuals. Those moments often make me stop and think, a little enviously, "Wow, that person just loves what they're doing!"

The first time I met Gunnar and heard him talk about Social Selling was definitely one of those moments. It made hiring Gunnar at Hootsuite an easy decision, where he poured that knowledge and passion into helping us recruit partners and customers, revamping our own Social Selling training curriculum and sharing his tips and tricks with several of our internal teams.

I'm thrilled to see that so many others will now benefit from Gunnar's knowledge and experience as well – you will not be disappointed!

Cybill Getgood

Chief Marketing Officer & Partner of TeamRecruit
(Newport Beach)

www.linkedin.com/in/cybillgetgood

I've had the honour to interview Gunnar Habitz in my podcast, and I knew then it would be just a matter of time till he launched his book about Social Selling.

Gunnar remarkably unpacks and distils the elements that exponentially grow your social presence into a sales engine. I especially love the pragmatic, step-by-step blueprint per chapter style that enables one to get started quickly.

If you are a sales leader or an executive who wants to increase your digital presence, influence, and captivate your audience, this book is for you. Ecstatic to see the many people this book will impact. Connect with Gunnar on LinkedIn and see for yourself!

Tom Williams

Chairman & Founder of Strategic Dynamics, co-author of "The Seller's Challenge" and "Buyer Centered Selling" (Scottsdale)

www.linkedin.com/in/thomasjwilliams

When I think of Gunnar Habitz, two images immediately come to my mind. Initially I think of a Social Selling expert and phenomenal content creator that routinely shares his knowledge and expertise on LinkedIn. His posts pique your interest, educate, inspire, entertain, and provoke further curiosity. As a reader you can't wait for his next illuminating narrative.

Second, and equally importantly, I think of someone with a thirst for knowledge who is passionate about ongoing professional development. He routinely devours books on sales, marketing, leadership, and strategy and then provides an in-depth analysis of each book, often along with detailed interviews with the author. This brings the content alive and further educates his followers.

Alex Wedderburn

Strategic Account Director at Hootsuite (New York)

www.linkedin.com/in/alex-wedderburn

Gunnar Habitz is a professional I have enjoyed knowing and working with for many years. Our unified passion for advocacy and Social Selling brought us together. Despite operating from two different continents, we often connected to share strategies, success stories, and with other individuals who were leading in this space

The best way I can describe Gunnar is that he is a true expert in his field, and I owe him so much of my success. This book will become a stable reference for the future of every professional engaged in Social Selling and Employee Advocacy.

Elaine Seeto
Director of Marketing APAC at GoTo
(Sydney)
www.linkedin.com/in/elaine-seeto

There is no doubt that Gunnar Habitz knows Social Selling and happily imparts his knowledge to benefit our colleagues at GoTo.

Through a "Winning with Social" session delivered for our APAC GoGetters, Gunnar provided framework and methodology to make Social Selling easy, and shared practical advice and best practices based on his personal experience and learnings, to build proficiency in Social Selling.

We're delighted to see tangible outcomes six weeks post the session, with more employees posting on LinkedIn, leading to 33% increase in employee engagement and 18% increase in reach on the posts shared!

I would like to congratulate Gunnar on the launch of *Connect & Act – Systematic Social Selling* and have no doubt it will deliver similarly impactful results to his readers.

Bassam Khoreich
Senior Customer Success Manager APAC at Wiz,
Member of Customer Success Collective (Sydney)
www.linkedin.com/in/bassamkhoreich

With a natural talent for social media networking, Gunnar has helped countless professionals achieve their goals by connecting them with the right people at the right time.

His Meetup events are legendary; packed with eager networkers and brimming with ideas, the perfect place to build valuable connections and find inspiration.

Gunnar has had an impressive career in the industry that has given him the expertise and experience to succeed in any situation. This book is a must-read for anyone looking to make it big in Social Selling.

Rema Lolas

Founder, CEO & Leadership Coach at Mind Matrix Coaching (Sydney)

www.linkedin.com/in/remalolas

Gunnar is no doubt one of the most passionate and knowledgeable people I know on the subject of Social Selling. His latest book, *Connect & Act*, is a practical handbook that emphasises the importance of building a brand and a network of genuine connections in the digital age, providing invaluable tips and techniques for leveraging social platforms effectively.

His passion and expertise shine through every page, as does his refreshing matter of fact-ness and provocative perspective. His tips and advice are practical and easy to implement to build your social presence and connect to meaningful relationships. With an engaging narrative and actionable insights, this book is an indispensable resource for anyone seeking to master and unlock the art of Social Selling! Congrats on your book!

Paul Bacanu

Global Channel Marketing Manager at Instructure (Gold Coast)

www.linkedin.com/in/paulbacanu

Social Selling has re-emerged into the spotlight after traditional marketing has flooded every corner of our life removing one of the most important elements, namely the positive connection between people that offer a service or goods and those who are keen to acquire them. It is this secret sauce that enables a person to build a stronger personal brand, strengthen client relationships and create lifelong customers.

Gunnar Habitz is a wizard who shares his experiences that forged this magic of Social Selling. I've been fortunate enough to work with Gunnar at events, participate as an avid student at his webinars, and it has helped me and my career tremendously.

Brent Marcombe
Founder and Managing Director of Growline Group Sales Training Consultancy (Melbourne)
www.linkedin.com/in/brentmarcombe

Over the 15 years I have had the pleasure of working with and building a friendship with Gunnar one thing has been abundantly clear: his genuine commitment to lifelong learning. As a widely published critic, author and sales leader, Gunnar has always gone the extra mile in developing the knowledge and skills of both himself and those around him. He now brings the same commitment to Social Selling.

Connect & Act – Systematic Social Selling is a must read for anyone who wants a clear and practical guide to building a targeted network that leads to meaningful conversations. Full of insightful tips from Gunnar and a host of other experts, this is a one-stop shop for Social Selling success. And the best of all? An open invitation from Gunnar to help support our ongoing Social Selling journey. An invitation I'll be certain to accept!

Jarrett Thomas
Chief Revenue Officer at OTB Digital, Keynote Speaker, Podcast Host of "More Than a Title" (New York)
www.linkedin.com/in/jarrettthomas1

I've had the pleasure of working with Gunnar, and he is someone who truly understands the importance of building relationships with potential customers and leveraging social media platforms to connect with them.

He is truly enthusiastic about using various social media channels to create meaningful conversations and engagement with prospects, and always exploring new ways to improve how he connects with customers.

Gunnar exemplifies and understands the value of being authentic and adding value to the conversation in order to build trust and establish long-term relationships with his potential clients.

CONNECT

&

ACT

SYSTEMATIC SOCIAL SELLING

A practical guide to using LinkedIn
for your profile, pleasure and profit

Gunnar Habitz

Edited by Karen Crombie, Exact Editing (Adelaide)
Cover by Josefina Luna, Drawtrip (Sydney)
Photos by the contributors; lightbulb and bookshelf images by Canva
Bricks image generated with BrickLink, trademark of LEGO® group (www.bricklink.com)

ISBN: 978-0-6458027-0-2 (Paperback)
ISBN: 978-0-6458027-1-9 (eBook)
ISBN: 978-0-6458027-2-6 (Kindle)
ISBN: 978-0-6458027-3-3 (Audiobook)
ISBN: 978-0-6458027-4-0 (Hardcover)
First published in Australia in 2023

Acknowledgement

Initially this book was going to be simply a summary of my best weekly blog episodes compiled quickly into an eBook. But as Social Selling is more about collaboration and engagement, I wanted to add more voices.

Thanks especially to the four experts who shared their wisdom in longer interviews: Roger Christie, Wendy Lloyd Curley, Scott Rogerson and Mark McInnes. Other professionals also added their highly appreciated expertise in shorter paragraphs across the book – many of them I know only from LinkedIn, others also in real life. The world is globally connected, so those experts are located across the US, in Canada, in the UK, in Europe and of course in Australia. Many of those professionals are also authors and you can find some of their books in the Cabinet section at the end.

At this stage I would like to mention those who helped me getting started with Social Selling: Sales Masterminds John Smibert and Tony J. Hughes, my coach Raul Kumar, and my mentor Joe Barnes. The learning from my Social Selling Sydney Meetup events, co-organised by Paul Bacanu, Tanya Jackman and Bassam Khoreich, turned into my online courses, thanks to the guidance of Amy Porterfield, Carl Parnell and Justin Welsh.

Of course I would like to acknowledge the participants in my regular LinkedIn Power Lab webinars and clients of my courses, thank you! Special appreciation goes to the teams of Hootsuite, Aircall, Adobe, and GoTo, who I've had the honour of share the principles of this book with, in various engagements or as part of my employment.

Finally I would like to thank Nicole Hasenmeile, Jane Jackson, and Sue Parker for supporting my professional journey with outstanding career advice to create our life Down Under.

This book and those I published before would have been impossible to write without the ongoing support of my wife Alexandra – my personal coach, hardest critic and best friend of 25 years!

Foreword

Raul Kumar

Founder & CEO of Resonate Business Ignition, helping businesses succeed through strategy, marketing and sales (Sydney)

www.linkedin.com/in/rkfromresonate

It is with tremendous pride, gratification and warmth that I type the foreword for *Connect & Act – Systematic Social Selling*, authored by my very dear friend, Gunnar Habitz. Our journey commenced years ago when I had the pleasure and privilege of mentoring Gunnar on the subject of Social Selling. As we traversed the ever-changing, evolving and developing terrain of digital sales together, our professional association matured into a treasured friendship.

In the context of the progressively digital and interpersonally linked sphere we inhabit, it's no surprise that conventional methodologies of B2B selling are being scrutinised and questioned. Gunnar, fortified with astute perception, keen insight, and unyielding devotion, has manifested as an extraordinary exemplar of Social Selling on a global stage. Comparable to the manner in which the concept of Social Selling has progressed over the years, Gunnar's tactics have similarly evolved. Through a series of trials and errors, we unearthed that the elusive key to triumph in B2B sales resides in the amalgamation of conventional B2B sales strategies and digital stratagems.

His book *Connect & Act – Systematic Social Selling* epitomises the zenith of Gunnar's copious experience and erudition, meticulously refined into an accessible compendium for professionals endeavouring to maintain a competitive edge in the domain of B2B sales. I state with confidence, that his knowledge and wisdom in the realm of digital selling will invigorate and illuminate those who immerse themselves within this book, learn from it, and apply the learnings in the physical and digital world.

As a coach and mentor to Gunnar, and being a dear friend of his, it is both fulfilling and humbling to bear witness to his growth and success. Gunnar's metamorphosis from an inquisitive learner to an established thought leader within the sphere of Social Selling is nothing short of extraordinary. His curiosity and aptitude to acclimate to what is new in the Social Selling landscape, and assess what yields success through consistent application, are attributes I have come to profoundly admire.

Throughout the years, Gunnar and I have engaged in innumerable dialogues, exchanged a multitude of concepts, and revelled in a plethora of victories. It is this synergistic spirit that has not only augmented our friendship but also further moulded our comprehension of the intricate realm of Social and Digital Selling. Together, Gunnar and I ascertained that combining the conventional with the disruptive, the tried and tested with the innovative, and the in-person approach with digital is the future of B2B sales.

Gunnar proffers a comprehensive and effective blueprint for harnessing the potency of Social Selling in his book. I take immense pride in having contributed to Gunnar's journey, and I am confident that this book will function as an invaluable asset for professionals navigating the sales landscape.

As you commence your personal expedition through the chapters of this book, I extend my warmest wishes for your profound success and enlightenment. May you, too, discover the consummate equilibrium between the conventional and the digital, and may your B2B sales ascend to unparalleled heights.

Gunnar, thanks ever so much for allowing me to be part of your journey. I have learnt a tremendous amount from you over the years; not just about social and digital selling, but also about business, about professional life, and about life, in general. Thank you for being a dear friend to me. I appreciate your presence in my life, mate. Thanks also for inviting me to write this foreword. It is an honour.

Contents

Instructions

This is my first book written in English, well knowing it's not my primary language. Living in Australia, I adopted a style close to British English with a few words borrowed from American English. My professional life at HP favoured American English but I changed that when moving to Australia, remembering my earlier times working in London.

This book has two functions: it is your guide to be read from beginning to end – and it also acts as a useful reference book when you want to come back for tips or when you are already advanced in your LinkedIn journey.

I decided not to use screenshots to show examples of subjects, as the visual aspect can change quickly. Instead, I explain the challenges of a topic, potential solutions, the benefits of solving them, plus four concrete tips to put the learning into action. That all fits neatly into a double page per topic for a bite-sized form of education.

At the end of each double page, you'll also find a link to respective landing pages about those topics. That is the place where you can find screenshots, further reading, or maybe a book tip. Combining a printed book with an online companion allows for updating the content without publishing a new version, saving you from buying another edition of the printed book when you already own it.

If you understand the broader principles about using professional media to advance your business agenda, you can also apply many key points of this book to the way you use Twitter, Facebook, Instagram or XING (the German equivalent to LinkedIn).

If you have any questions, please let me know – I am always happy to help and improve the book for the next edition!

Start

Clarity

"I guarantee the clarity of your content is its biggest quality."

Jasmin (Jay) Alić

Dear reader,

Welcome to my book, *Connect & Act – Systematic Social Selling*! Much appreciated that you decided to learn about my favourite topic.

This book is much more than just a compilation of my weekly blogging series on LinkedIn using the hashtag #socialsellingmonday. It's a comprehensive guide to all I've learned about practicing and teaching the craft.

Soon after moving to Australia in 2016, I observed that some corporate employees were using Social Selling activities with the purpose of supporting the buying journey of their prospective clients. I realised that most people were totally passive on the platform, as they didn't understand LinkedIn's move from a job search tool into the content ecosystem it is today.

Just one user segment was totally missing back then: small business professionals. This was the time before life coaches, beauty therapists and all kinds of consultants discovered LinkedIn and before clever content creators with massive followings appeared in our feeds.

I had the privilege to learn from influencers and sales coaches Tony J. Hughes, John Smibert, and Raul Kumar, who became my coach back in 2017. As a former sales trainer with a passion for enablement, I started a blogging series about Social Selling with the intention to write just a handful of episodes. While typing this, I just published week 222, and I'm still counting!

Sharing what I learned with a "lifelong learning" approach, I published my first free email course, to entice those professionals in small to mid-sized businesses to be more active. I improved the profiles of users, from financial advisers to not-for-profit professionals, and created my first online course.

This book covers what I learned about the organic side of social media for personal profiles – we won't go into paid advertising, company pages or hiring people using the job-related functions of the platform. Each of the double pages has a link for further reading. You can read it from beginning to end but also come back to any double page for reference. Enjoy!

Definition

Please allow me to start with a bit of clarity as the term Social Selling might not be obvious to everyone. It is actually not about *selling* as such, despite the misleading name.

Some experts like inbound marketing company HubSpot mentioned that "Social Selling is when salespeople use social media to interact directly with their prospects." What do you think of this definition; true or false?

In my view it's not entirely wrong, but far from the full potential. And it shouldn't be the only method to reach customers. HubSpot provided more insight: "Salespeople will provide value by answering prospect's questions and offering thoughtful content until the prospect is ready to buy."

That sounds much better as it contains the word *value*. When shared content is tailored for the prospective customer, then it becomes *perceived value* in the eyes of the prospect. These days buyers research much more by themselves online, involving potential suppliers much later. Being active online and on social media helps to grab their attention earlier.

What do you think of my own definition?

> *"Social Selling is a clever approach of using social media*
> *and digital tools to enhance business conversations."*

In my view we add both social and digital tools to our existing instruments in changing combinations, depending on the situation. This way we reach the critical milestone to *take a conversation offline* into a call or a meeting to *advance your business agenda*, the universal target of Social Selling.

Enjoy reading this book – and please share your feedback!

Gunnar

Bricks

Occasionally I talk about LEGO® in my webinars and my blog posts. I like distilling a problem into building blocks to understand patterns before coming up with solution ideas. When I moved to Sydney, the first souvenir I bought was the famous Sydney Opera House as a LEGO® brick set. The real Opera House looked quite close to my model!

The four major chapters of this book depend on each other. The first one is called *Complete* on purpose because we're focusing on bringing your personal brand on LinkedIn up to a great level. It won't ever be perfect, so we'll come back to it regularly, maybe every quarter or so. The three following chapters *Connect*, *Content*, and *Convert* are also ongoing tasks which you can see in a constant loop.

Many professionals want to become more active on LinkedIn and update their digital presence but it feels as if the task is equal to a tower of unsorted LEGO® bricks – you have no idea where to start and how they all fit together. The different elements and possible combinations need some guidance.

Here is my Social Selling concept modelled as a builder with LEGO® bricks: Complete (red) is a tall element with six studs facing to the right. I don't erect the bricks in a vertical direction because the timeline of our activities on LinkedIn is going to be represented in a horizontal flow.

The other three elements, Connect (blue), Content (yellow), and Convert (green), have only two studs each but are built using double-height bricks. The square area covers four single bricks, each representing the most important points of each element.

We can now attach all three elements in a row to the long one to get a complete block, representing the ongoing loop of Connect, Content, and Convert on the same level.

Have a look on the next page at how it all comes together, shown with a white brick representing the rough ashlar as the starting point.

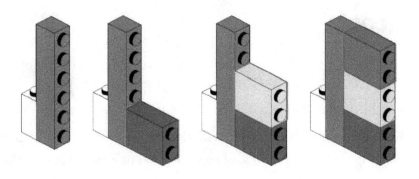

(images generated with BrickLink, trademark of LEGO® group, www.bricklink.com)

In the following time period such as a week we add a further three bricks to it to document the regular activities. After a quarter or even longer, we add another red Complete element with six studs for a quick check of our profile. This provides the stability we need for the future.

What do these LEGO® bricks represent?

- **Complete**: Purpose, Basic, Details, Advanced, Extras, Reflection
- **Connect**: Network, Connection, Support, Attitude
- **Content**: Participate, Prepare, Post, Perform
- **Convert**: Plan, Communication, Mindset, Results

This is a simplified version of the following chapters showing you how the topics of Social Selling are interconnected. There are various ways you can create your own set of bricks and advance it further as you go.

Good luck in becoming your own architect and builder at the same time. If you need any help, please let me know.

Concept

Turning a passive profile into an active attraction requires a couple of ingredients. I describe them in the shape of four LEGO® bricks fixed to each other in the proper direction.

We start with the first brick as a vertical tower. This first regular step in Social Selling represents your digital representation or personal brand. Not everyone is comfortable showing their true self to strangers in the online space, I understand that. But if we want to make the most of professional social media platforms, we need to show at least one version of ourselves online.

Does it have to be our true self? Maybe not. But the more authentically we show who we are, the more likely that other professionals will perceive us as someone they know, like, and trust.

The online world is not about facts, it's all about perception.

Once we've climbed that vertical tower, successfully aligning perception and facts, we add the other steps in a horizontal direction next to it. They are longer than the first step but not as high.

The second regular step is all about finding the right people and connecting with them. Have you heard the saying, "You never have a second chance to make a first impression?" When we tap into the attention of someone who we haven't meet yet, we need to manage this unique chance in a proper manner so that they want to connect with us. This second step repeats on a daily or at least weekly basis.

The third regular step is all about content. LinkedIn would still be just an online CV, if they didn't acquire the content platform Pulse. Back then we would just provide a status update or read long-format articles from others.

Today, we have various ways in which to play with content, either as a post (the former status update), an article in stand-alone fashion or even as a regular newsletter. There are so many options, like image posts or text posts, engaging carousels, live videos, and even polls.

The fourth and often underestimated step builds the bridge to the initial reason why we are active on LinkedIn in the first place: we want to convert a conversation towards advancing our business agenda.

That conversion goal will be different for everyone: sales professionals want to help customers and earn a commission from the revenue gained. Marketing teams would like to raise brand awareness. Not-for-profit organisations seek donations and to form collaborations. Educational institutions are seeking overseas students or to improve their reputation as a centre for research. And HR teams want to position themselves to attract talent.

If we connect all our bricks in the proper order with a constant loop, we will improve our Social Selling activities and gain consistent results.

Here are my steps connecting the whole journey along the LEGO® bricks:

1. **Complete**: Get started aligning online perception and facts in your digital representation. This includes your personal brand online as well as your vision, mission, and values.

2. **Connect**: Follow influential professionals in your industry or connect directly with them. Build your network constantly and periodically delete those you don't need anymore.

3. **Content**: Comment on their posts, share some of their work to your network with an introduction revealing why that particular piece is important to your tribe, adding your personal view.

4. **Convert**: Discuss topics directly with those who react to your content or comments. This way you can advance those chats into serious business conversations.

This book follows the principle of those four steps which you can follow from A to Z, or you can read each individual topic like a reference.

 www.connectandactbook.com/concept

Background

Obsession – this word represents an ideal motivator to follow something with a burning desire. Perhaps a task in your job to win a promotion, a special hobby, or supporting a volunteering cause close to your heart.

Back in Europe I used LinkedIn to connect with professionals locally and later in my international role (and XING for the German-speaking market). For me it started out as more of a Rolodex to capture my contacts; I would never have posted any content. I didn't even have an About section – or Summary as it was called back then.

That changed when I first attended a two-month leadership program in Sydney. Soon I realised that LinkedIn played a stronger role Down Under to connect locally and with the world. As I started to enjoy networking events as an important way to build my tribe, it became an obsession to learn more about using social media activities to broaden my network and help others.

I had never heard about the term Social Selling back then! That changed when I met John Smibert from the Sales Masterminds group who just launched the Sales Executive event series with remarkable keynote speakers. One of them was Tony J. Hughes, the author of my favourite sales book, *The Joshua Principle*. John and Tony talked about Social Selling a lot and pointed me to Raul Kumar, an excellent practitioner. Attending his Executive program further opened my eyes.

At the end of 2018 I started a weekly blogging series on LinkedIn targeting small businesses instead of the corporate employees where the term came from. Using the hashtag #socialsellingmonday, I've posted about it every week for more than 4.5 years, always indicating four practical steps per topic.

That obsession evolved into my role at the famous Social Selling software vendor Hootsuite, where I updated their professional course, too. And afterwards I became a Social Selling practitioner at GoTo.

Chapter 1

Complete

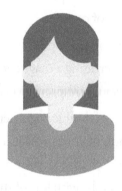

"Your personal brand is what people say about you when you are not in the room."

Chris Ducker

Your Personal Brand

Our Social Selling journey starts with your personal brand, which is basically the online version of who you are – or how you want to present yourself to your audience.

In the earlier days of LinkedIn it was easy: you were just *role at company*. This was followed by a bullet point list of responsibilities job by job. After all, you only updated it when changing roles, otherwise you wouldn't log into the platform at all.

Over time, LinkedIn became *the* personal branding platform based on content to gain engagement. The profile information is a nice add-on to show who created that piece of content.

This chapter covers my top tips on how to showcase and constantly improve your personal brand, creating a magnetic profile which enhances your digital reputation and adds suitable professionals into your network.

I have chosen the format of double pages per topic to show where you can boost the current status quo of your profile. This layout was chosen to give you a chance to target and change smaller areas quickly instead of going through a long list of paragraphs with lots of theory.

What most professionals need is an understanding of challenges, suggestions on how to change, with a background on why that area is worth improving, then some examples and relevant benefits. This is exactly how all the double pages in this book are designed.

When I came to Sydney to study the Advanced Diploma of Management and Leadership, I had to adapt to a lot at once. A great help at that time was a book from Joshua Waldman with bite-size chunks along with 30 common profile mistakes. The concept of that small book enticed me to quickly put that learning into action.

That is what I would like you to do as well. When you realise that you want to change something, then hit pause, stop reading and act!

Your personal brand on LinkedIn and other social media platforms starts with having a completed profile. You want to utilise the most relevant fields to paint a picture as the genuine and caring person you are.

Right here is the first challenge: whether we're shy or good storytellers, talking about ourselves is often difficult. It's even more so when we need to write our About section in the first person when we don't like bragging!

I suggest reading some well-written profiles by people you know and then comparing that with the impression you have about them. To find those good examples as a guide for yourself, ask professionals (not necessarily family members) about how they describe you in order to find the right words.

There are mainly three ways in which people visit your profile: they can look for your name exactly, they can search for a provider of a product or service, or they learn about you from the content you shared or engaged with. In order to be found, we must optimise our profile, especially for the second search mentioned, when readers don't know about us yet.

In this chapter we talk about the profile itself, covering the first two ways of how someone can land on your LinkedIn profile. To be clear, not your LinkedIn page – the platform differentiates between the *profile* of professionals, indicated by a rounded picture, compared to the *page* of a company, which has a square image with completely different fields and functions. The focus of this book is profiles, not company pages.

There are various reasons to improve your LinkedIn profile. Many only adopt it with a job change or promotion. Entrepreneurs want to stand out, to be found and gain clients constantly. In all cases it starts with finding clarity about your personal brand: that means your story, your differentiator, your values – and you have only one chance to make a first impression.

Employees and entrepreneurs have one thing in common: they describe *who* they help to achieve *what* by providing *what type of service*.

Interview with Roger Christie

Roger and I first met on LinkedIn by engaging with each other's content over a couple of months before finally meeting in a café on the Northern Beaches in Sydney. Since then we've talked regularly about leadership, social media and digital reputation, the topic of his insightful podcast.

His company Propel especially helps top leaders from listed companies in Australia with their approach to shaping their digital footprint. His team of experts adds further research for certain situations such as elections and the impact from the pandemic.

Roger Christie
Founder & Managing Director at Propel, podcast host of "Your Digital Reputation" (Sydney)
www.linkedin.com/in/rogerchristie

How do you define Social Selling?

For me, Social Selling has always been more about *social* and less about *selling*. What I mean by that is embracing the fundamental principles of listening, building relationships, collaborating, and creating shared value for people. If you do these things well and use social media to scale your efforts, the selling takes care of itself.

Could you please share examples of positive engagement from top leaders after they became visible on social media?

There are so many. Way back in 2012 I was working with an executive who decided to get more active on LinkedIn as a way to build new relationships. Within months of posting and engaging with others he'd landed a six-figure deal.

More recently, I know leaders who've attracted key talent simply by posting content that reflects and amplifies their values. And others who've made staff feel welcomed and valued by sending them connection requests, rather than remaining hidden in their ivory tower. When the CEO takes the time to connect with you, you know you belong.

What are the challenges associated with digital reputation risk?

Propel released a report recently looking at ASX200 CEOs' use of LinkedIn. Almost 85% were invisible, inactive, or ineffective. The real risk is avoidance, not participation. When you avoid social media, you let others control the narrative around your reputation, you leave competitors to be heard while you stay silent, and you lose a vital direct communication channel in times of crisis.

There is no risk to participation, provided an executive understands how to use social media themselves – and their advisors provide regular insights on stakeholder sentiment and workflows to make any efforts sustainable.

What is your top tip to encourage leaders to become visible online?

We have a methodology at Propel called "The Five Drivers of Digital Reputation" (PPLAN). The first 'P' and cornerstone of the five drivers is Purpose. The reason it sits at the core of the other four drivers – Profile, Listening, Activity, and Network – is that Purpose should inform everything a leader does.

The best thing a leader can do – to save time, to mitigate risk, to increase their impact, and to feel confident – is to define their Purpose; their 'why' for turning up on social media. An hour spent bedding that down will save them considerable time – and potential pain – in the future. Never just 'do social' because everyone else is – define your why by considering your organisational goals alongside your personal passions and stakeholder needs. That's what makes a leader stand out online.

Purpose

Did you ever describe the purpose behind your professional activities or communicate the motivation behind all you do? Is it an inner calling for your profession? Maybe your family were craftsmen for generations? Or you changed your career completely from a corporate employee to becoming your own boss or you founded a start-up company?

There are many different reasons to find your purpose that drives you as person. Being able to articulate that in the form of a story helps to describe the purpose, in your personal brand in general and on LinkedIn as one way to inspire others by your unique approach to your profession.

The challenge from the point of view of your profile readers? In most cases they can't see any trace of such a purpose. The majority of LinkedIn profiles still show the old format of an online CV without a special drive or anything that lets them stand out. It's a sea of sameness.

Do we want to show our purpose in the first place? Is it not enough to be known as the plumber of that region as customers consistently thank us for a job well done, regardless of what motivates us? Think about that as a buyer of a service. If you only want to solve a customer's problem in the form of a commodity, then you miss the chance to show what makes you unique – even if your current role might not require that. But one day it will, one day you must show your purpose to the world. And LinkedIn is the place for that!

Steve Jobs talked about purpose as the driver behind the work we do in his Stanford Commencement Address in 2005: "Your work is going to fill a large part of your life and the only way to be truly satisfied is to do what you believe is great work. And the only way to do great work is to love what you do."

Many companies declare their purpose on another level than the typical vision, mission, and values statements. Here is a relatable example of purpose from LinkedIn: "Connect the world's professionals to make them more productive and successful."

Switching back to our own personal brand, I like Tijmen Rümke's four building blocks of purpose as described in his article "The 4 Drivers of Purpose in your Life" on Medium:

- Passion: what you love doing
- Mastery: what you're really good at
- Values: what you find important
- Mission: what you want to build in your life

These four drivers obviously overlap on your inward journey. I agree with his closing statement: "The higher your mission and the deeper your meaning, the further it can reach and resonate with other people."

These are my steps to define the purpose for your personal brand:

1. **Understand** your personal unique value proposition (UVP) by asking yourself what you stand for, what your values are, and what you contribute differently to your target market.

2. **Draft** a few examples with a structure like "I help A to do B" to get started. You might add "by doing C" or "to achieve D" to be more concrete. Show that to those who know what you do.

3. **Craft** your personal branding statement as a one or two-sentence phrase which acts as your slogan. Show the outcome of your work in the view of the reader.

4. **Align** your purpose and thoughts about your personal branding with your company or organisation to ensure both are perceived as compatible. Easy for solopreneurs, still possible for employees.

Once you have noted your purpose as the base for everything else, it will be easier to complete the following parts such as the Headline and About sections and even the paragraphs for the Experience area.

☞ www.connectandactbook.com/purpose

Headline

Do you want to copy the average profiles of those who categorise themselves in unremarkable ways? Are you a mere electrician, plumber, family lawyer, mortgage broker, or salesperson? I suspect that you feel that you're much more than that and would like to showcase it well.

But look at the text on your business card; that indeed complies with the basic, short job description. Fortunately, we have more choices in how to describe our personal brand on LinkedIn.

Those who started early on the platform from the old online CV days of LinkedIn might still list "job at company" as their headline. In my view this is far too stereotyped and doesn't say anything about you, the value you bring to the market, how you help others to achieve their fulfilment at work or in their personal life. We are more than that!

The headline is not just placed under your LinkedIn profile, it is visible with each post you write and even under each comment you make. The first 60 characters are the most important, given the short space on the mobile app when commenting.

How to create the ideal headline? I distinguish three ways to craft an elegant headline for your personal brand. Have a look at these examples:

1. Role at company like Paddy Srinivasan: *Chief Executive Officer at GoTo.* I would keep this only for the top leadership roles of well-known organisations with descriptive titles.

2. Outcome-related description like Justin Welsh: *The Diversified Solopreneur | Building a portfolio of one-person businesses to $5M in revenue. Posts & articles about the process.* Works best when bringing others to the journey with stated results.

3. Mixing highlights and descriptions like Raul Kumar: *Founder & CEO | Helping B2B businesses grow through Strategy, Marketing & Sales.* Remarkable intro under each comment.

Here is my earlier example mixing those descriptions: When I worked at the Australian Risk Management software vendor, I replaced *Channel Sales Manager at Noggin* with *Helping consultants, partners and their clients manage risk smarter | Alliance & Channel Manager | Social Media Mentor.*

This is a combination of the target audience (consultants and partners), company slogan (*manage risk smarter*), searchable keywords (*Alliance* and *Channel Manager*) and my social media passion at the end. When I added the word *Alliance*, my feed changed as LinkedIn started to show me a range of other Alliance Managers and their content to engage with.

These are my suggestions to finetune your headline:

1. **Research** how your market companions and others in adjacent areas describe themselves in their headline. Brainstorm words for you that cut through the noise while remaining familiar.

2. **Ask** others around you how they describe you and what you offer to the market. This way you can get an external view with suitable word suggestions you can use for your headline.

3. **Craft** two or three headlines combining an outcome and some keywords with a vertical separator. Show these examples to your ideal target market and others who know you well.

4. **Adapt** your headline with the winning suggestion and check how it looks like when you post and comment. Finetune until you are happy and the result withstands external comparison.

The right headline helps you to escape the ordinary, to show what you can do for others, to entice people to watch your profile and engage with your content. Does it look better than the standard approach which most of your competitors still use? Convinced to change it right now? Go!

☞ www.connectandactbook.com/headline

Visuals

How many seconds does a person take to read your profile and make a decision to move on or to take an action like following or even sending a connection request? Maybe less than ten seconds? One of the most critical elements are the visual components: the profile photo and the background image behind.

I often wonder why even executives in larger companies often use private photos taken by amateurs for their digital presence without any reflection on how that photo represents them. In most of these cases the light and shadow is really bad, many others have contrast issues or are even blurry.

This is not Facebook or Instagram. Even if you work in a fancy job, a photo in a more casual setting should still look professional, representing your carefully created personal brand on LinkedIn.

There are so many sources for finding a good portrait photographer for this type of professional photo. Many larger conferences even have a booth with a chance to get your photo done for free. Or you can walk into any photo studio – you can even combine a session with official photos you need anyway, such as for your passport or other government documents.

Think about your branded colours for a moment. If you like the photo you've got but not the colours behind you, then you can easily remove that background in the free tool www.remove.bg to download a transparent photo in PNG format. Then you can add a background layer in the likewise free Canva (www.canva.com) with the desired colours or other visual effects.

The next element is the background image. Currently the size of a profile background is 1584 x 396 pixels, basically a 4:1 aspect ratio. If you upload an image in another ratio between length and height, LinkedIn has to adjust and cut on either side. Better you go to Canva and design that whole background image from scratch. Keep in mind that the bottom left part will be overlapped by your profile photo.

What else should we add to that image? If you search for examples from others, you will find the best creativity from content creators like Jasmin (Jay) Alić who writes the outcome of his work in clear letters in the image. Some add a little arrow pointing to the bell right below the background image, requesting readers to click there to be notified for new posts. Well done!

Those in corporate roles often have to use company-supplied images without any chance to modify them. Find out what is possible without violating any rules. The personal brand is yours even if the company pays for your subscription. I believe in a mutual benefit so be mindful of the possibilities.

Here are my steps to improve the visual aspects of your profile:

1. **Request** a new profile headshot be taken as your existing photo might be either too old or doesn't show you in the right light. The first impression counts!

2. **Ask** the photographer to take several photos in the same setting as you can use those for other areas on LinkedIn, especially if you want to combine them later with content carousels.

3. **Design** the background image based on a clever combination of visual elements and text to showcase your capabilities, well aligned with the colours of your personal or company brand.

4. **Use** modern tools like Photo Feeler to request feedback about the perception of your chosen images (www.photofeeler.com) or let AI create a headshot from your selfies (www.tryitonai.com).

Now that your profile photo and background images are refreshed, compare your LinkedIn presence with others in your field. Don't you agree that it looks so much more appealing to click into your profile now and find out more about the person behind the image?

☞ www.connectandactbook.com/visuals

About

Which is the most difficult part to write within your LinkedIn profile? That section which takes the longest time to complete and in most cases will be the last part you touch at all? The About section, which used to be called the Summary. That is no surprise as we are taught not to brag about ourselves. Even the best authors typically write better about someone else.

As I mentioned earlier, LinkedIn is *not* your online CV and also *not* your online resumé. Those words are often used interchangeably, but the CV is more academic with details while the resumé is a shorter summary of roles with responsibilities and achievements.

A compelling About section is written in the first person, not in the third. It is a written form of an elevator pitch which lasts for a couple of minutes. Imagine you are invited to speak at an event where everyone has a minute to introduce themselves. Surely nobody would talk about themselves in the third person. The same applies here: we write about ourselves.

The About section is the best place for a first impression beyond the visual elements, giving you the opportunity to tell more about yourself. You can use it to highlight your career choices in context, share some of your proudest achievements, or describe other relevant elements of your personality which are not visible job by job. Especially if you've moved around industries or even countries, as in my case, it is worth mentioning there to tell your story.

Later in this book we'll discuss a major challenge for content writers: staring at a blank screen often prevents you from getting started crafting your words. Using examples or templates can sometimes be helpful. Therefore I list some useful examples in the link at the bottom of this topic which LinkedIn itself recommends.

How long should the summary be, you might ask? I suggest four to five paragraphs of not more than five lines each. Please keep the mobile reader in mind – nothing is worse than scrolling through a big block of text on a device.

Your summary should show you in the best light as possible. This is not about boasting about why you are the best at the job. Think about the culture of an organisation; how do you fit in the place where you work, the job function or industry? What makes you tick as a sales professional?

The most important task is getting the first sentence right as this makes the reader curious to continue learning about you as an approachable person. In the middle part you can add a famous quote that resonates with you or add a challenging question to the reader. Conclude the About section with a call-to-think, mentioning which problem you solve and what you do for others.

These are my tips to craft a remarkable summary:

1. **Brainstorm** about those topics you want to include. Check how others in your field describe themselves. List important keywords you want to include with the reader in mind, not a machine.

2. **Craft** a bullet point structure of your About section to see the flow on screen or on paper. Insert storytelling elements that show what makes you stand out. Add strong statements as well.

3. **Ask** colleagues or business partners instead of close friends how they perceive you, what makes it unique to work with you in their view. They might mention words you wouldn't find otherwise.

4. **Write** your own story in a couple of paragraphs using the bullet point structure and the feedback you received from others. Print that and read it out loud. Does it sound like you? Great!

Well done – you updated your existing About section or took these pages as a trigger to write yours from scratch. Believe me, you will never be fully satisfied with the result. You always find the About section of others more compelling. Get used to it and update yours regularly.

☞ www.connectandactbook.com/about

Expertise

When LinkedIn was used mostly as a job search tool, most people only updated their experience in a similar way to how they would list it in their CV. You can still see the majority of professionals showing bullet points of their responsibilities, rarely with achievements added. If yours looks like that, it is time to change that. Now.

There are various sections where you can show your expertise in your field. The first place is the **Experience** section. Instead of using a boring list of responsibilities, I suggest crafting three paragraphs: The first will be about the company (not everyone might know them) and your area. When I worked at market leading company HP (Hewlett-Packard) I explained my products and territory as an introduction.

The second paragraph outlined my role in a non-jargon description which would be clearly understood by the target audience. I replaced internal role titles with terms well-known in the industry. The third paragraph talked about my achievements. It can be a list but free text is better.

LinkedIn likes to show progression within a company when you add a new role and end the earlier position without a break. That underlines that you can grow and advance as a professional at your workplace.

The following area introduces your **Education**. When your universities or schools are well-known, they should have their own page on LinkedIn and then it shows their logo. Beyond a degree you can also list special projects or other achievements as long they are relevant to your career. No need to list all activities, especially if these occurred a long time ago.

If you have a bachelor's or master's degree, I suggest not listing your high school, college, etc. unless it is a famous school and you want to connect with fellow alumni. Feel free to leave out mentioning the years you attended if you don't want to reveal your age. In my case I left out studying Computer Science as courses in the '90s were not on the same level as today.

While education is backwards related and we use LinkedIn in the present to work towards a bright future, the section **Licences & certifications** shows more current achievements. Those in a technical field will want to add their certificates from the likes of Microsoft, Salesforce, Hootsuite, etc. Those often come with credentials from third-party tools as real proof, sometimes even with a link or an expiry date to refresh afterwards.

You can add further professional education in the **Courses** section. That includes those further development activities which are not accompanied with an official licence as those mentioned above. You can also list **languages** and respective **test scores** in their sections.

These are my suggestions to update your expertise:

1. **Check** how others in your field describe their work experience. It may take a while to find outstanding descriptions to learn from, potentially requiring you to look into adjacent industries.

2. **Transform** your current experience section from a bullet point list into an outcome-related description with a few paragraphs. Be clear about the achievements in a non-bragging way.

3. **Adjust** the education section to be clear what you achieved and to keep the most relevant degree. Feel free to add details about the thesis you wrote as long it is relevant to your career.

4. **Add** further professional development to show your interest in lifelong learning by listing respective certificates from external sources and other courses along your journey.

Congratulations! Your expertise looks much better after applying the tips listed above to transition from an online CV (which nobody reads anyway) into a humble, engaging description of your capabilities in context.

☞ www.connectandactbook.com/expertise

Credibility

You want to be perceived as the genuine and caring person you are, ideally proven by others to avoid talking about yourself too much. This has been difficult enough in the About section! Let's go through the relevant areas of your profile where external proof supports your personal brand.

The most advanced way to read about someone's expertise, impact and character are the **Recommendations**. Requesting this from a person you know means quite an effort from them and should be done only when both of you worked together for sufficient time to showcase the influence of the receiver. While it is not good practice to respond quickly with a counter recommendation as it looks like a deal, a degree of give and take is normal.

The easier way to endorse someone is when you vouch for their capabilities is the **Skills** section. With a maximum of 50 skills available, you can add relevant keywords typical to your industry or personal development. If you add some and save, LinkedIn will suggest others suitable to your individual situation. You can add three of them in the top part of that section. Endorsing someone occasionally is for me a clever way to say hello.

If you are a writer in an academic collaboration or for business, you can add finished titles into the **Publications** section along with mentioning co-authors and a link to the respective book. I suggest using this only for serious publications, not just a short article in an online magazine.

The next section to show credibility is **Honors & Awards**. We want to be careful as to how we use that section as it doesn't require any external proof. A typical example especially for sales professionals is being chosen for the annual President Club award for outstanding sales performance.

Further to this, you can include the respective **Organisations** which count you as member to underline your broader interests beyond work. In my case, it is the Sales Enablement Society, the Chartered Manager Institute in the UK, plus IML in ANZ and National Trust Australia.

Do you contribute to your community with any volunteering work or have you done so in the past? You can add this to your profile as well in the **Volunteering** section. It looks quite similar to the work experience as it contains the name of an organisation, your role as well as start and end dates. You can choose one of 15 different causes, from Animal Welfare, Education and Health to Veteran Support. A short description can show the impact of your work for the greater good in a local or global environment.

I love contributing to the educational space so here I listed my mentorship in Australia and India as well as supporting animal welfare programs in Asian and African countries.

There is a dedicated **Causes** section about your caring interests as well.

These are my ideas to add credibility to your personal brand:

1. **Request** recommendations from people in your network who can vouch for your mutual experience. Suggest receiving one and giving one per quarter, also do this outside of job changes.

2. **Fill** your skills list towards at least 40 with those suitable for your job type and industry. I recommend checking the skill selection of your colleagues, partners and competitors as well.

3. **Complete** any other achievements in your work in the view of your network, including awards and publications, without being perceived as boasting.

4. **Show** that you care about the greater good by adding your current or former volunteering work or your participation in respective organisations.

Well done; now your readers can get a better understanding of the credible and serious professional you are.

☞ www.connectandactbook.com/credibility

Keywords

Simplicity is key when it comes to using keywords on social media. You can give them a theme or find another way to relate them to you.

Our digital presence has various functions: for those who know us, it should display our activities. For those who seek a professional based on their required context, keywords are the essential elements to find us.

The only tricky thing: where should we embed those keywords on LinkedIn (and other social media platforms)? I've seen many professionals who place them in the headline, very much like pitching. Certainly a good place, as long it doesn't sound too salesy.

The best place for keywords within the profile beyond the shared content is the About section. Craft insightful sentences with those words to be read as a human, not in a CV bullet point approach. We should have in mind that LinkedIn is well optimised for Search Engine Optimisation (SEO) so it can be found on Google, not just within LinkedIn.

The good thing: you can declare some keywords per season or major event. If you change your role or function, if your company has a massive shift like mergers or acquisitions, or even at the beginning of a new year you can even declare those keywords in your content. Just make sure the About section is updated accordingly.

To show an example, here are mine, which I declared at the beginning of this year: collaboration, contribution, compassion, and consistency. These words are part of my personal brand and my values – and represent good business conduct for so many.

You can create relevant content suitable to your target market by commenting, curating or creating your own material embedding your keywords. Don't forget this: **Consistent content converts into conversations.** The benefit of using those within LinkedIn is two-fold: you can be found based on yours – and you can also search well within the platform.

Here's an example: Once I was asked to fill a panel at a Risk Management conference with three experts. One person in my network had a well-written profile so I found him easily. But who else should I offer the panel seats to?

I used my earlier content as a way to find the other two. I remembered that I'd posted about a problem worth solving from a risk standpoint which received around 20 comments. Using the right terms ("emergency management" and "incident" in this case), I easily found that post again, along with the professionals who shared their views. Then it was a simple matter to send direct messages to them and eventually they spoke at the event.

These four areas within LinkedIn help you to search for keywords as long they are placed well in advance.

1. **Messages**: If you added a personal message for an invitation using a keyword like the name of an event, you can find all messages relevant to that keyword.

2. **Content**: Click into the Search bar at the top and press Enter without any word, then the button 'Posts' to fine tune your search (as well as 'Companies,' 'Courses,' 'Services' etc).

3. **People**: From that search bar click on 'People' and 'All filters' before going further into detail. If the choices are not enough, you can find more inside LinkedIn Sales Navigator.

4. **Hashtags**: If you want to ensure people follow your posts, create your own hashtag with your name or keyword like I did for my series #socialsellingmonday, which helps a lot to find content.

If you start finding people or content, you will shift your own behaviour and start planting the seeds of a future search by placing relevant keywords beforehand as you know they will be used one day in the future.

☞ www.connectandactbook.com/keywords

Creators

Do you remember when LinkedIn was only a job search engine? Later it became a corporate Rolodex with most company employees creating their accounts and then forgetting about them.

That time is over. LinkedIn is now driven by content creators. We connect not just with people we know but also with those we *want* to have in our network based on their content. And I want you to be part of this movement.

But to participate we need to elevate your creative juice to the next level. Creativity shows the difference between most people just consuming content on LinkedIn and those active professionals contributing with their own or curated material.

Let us think for a moment about our target audience. They can reach us in one of three possible ways: either searching for a specific person, looking for someone who covers a certain role, or finding content on a given topic. It's the same in real life when we are looking for a service provider of an outcome, such as a hairdresser, business coach, beautician, or mortgage broker. We are looking for an outcome and engage the person who we believe can deliver that in the best possible way according to our requirements.

Unfortunately, most LinkedIn profiles still have the same old structure from the days of an online CV. The Featured area near the About section was the first attempt to provide a place to showcase more interesting material.

LinkedIn introduced the so-called Creator Mode especially for those who want to use the platform to build a personal brand based on the content they share. We could say that they are keen to get a share of what would otherwise be posted as a blog on a website elsewhere. In any case, it is a good move because engaging content helps to convert towards great conversations!

If you want to see the Creator Mode in action, you'll recognise the profiles of those creators as they show up to five hashtags below their headline. This acts as a quick check preview of what they are talking about.

The purpose of the Creator Mode is getting conversations going based on engaging material. This is more about gaining followers than collecting more direct connections (limited to 30,000). Therefore the blue button below the profile changes in the view of a stranger from 'Connect' to 'Follow'. And the order of the profile structure changes as well: the Activity section with a selection of posts now comes before the About section.

There is a hidden benefit of perception: profiles with Creator Mode look more vibrant. We assume they are constantly sharing useful material which apparently others engage with.

This is how you can get the Creator Mode for your profile to highlight your content and get more conversations going:

1. **Switch** it on in the Resources section of your profile, as long you have at least 150 followers and a good standing at LinkedIn which basically qualifies nearly everyone.

2. **Define** up to five hashtags you talk about which are followed by many professionals (my hashtags are #innovation, #leadership, #management, #workfromhome, and #socialselling).

3. **Use** some of the dedicated creator tools such as the newsletter (please subscribe to mine called "Learn From Books"), LinkedIn Live or the new Audio Event feature.

4. **Continue** sharing your content regularly to enjoy more relevant followers who will most likely engage with your material (and of course you will pay back the favour and comment on theirs).

Your consistency in sharing content as a Creator will be rewarded with higher engagement from new followers, and their content can bring you to the next idea and into conversations you wouldn't have otherwise.

☞ www.connectandactbook.com/creators

Featured

Your best performing post with the largest number of views? Maybe it was a couple of months ago. The post you are most proud of? It's also not visible anymore. And what about that post with the highest engagement? They are all out of sight. Let's bring them to light again.

Your LinkedIn profile allows declaring some of your posts as 'featured' in the form of a carousel. For members using the Creator Mode, the Featured area is placed between the sections Highlights and Activity to place relevant content as high as possible. Others without Creator Mode will find it further down if they have declared a post or link as 'featured' at all.

With so much content available it is a massive challenge to remember and show the most important pieces we ever posted. Likewise it is difficult for our readers to find them easily. This is solved better with those lengthy articles as they are all placed nicely in order. But most professionals never use them.

It is very easy to declare a certain post as 'featured'. Just go to the three dots on the top right of any post and click on the first option: 'Feature on top of profile'. Then it becomes the furthest item on the right in the list. Good thing: you can also feature a link to an external website, not only posts inside LinkedIn. You can even upload the link to a video.

That carousel includes five of those items with three of them visible on the desktop version and just one on the mobile app. You can scroll to the right to get a good understanding of what the person declares as their best work. After scrolling to those five items, you receive a list. You can remove any items from the Featured list with the click of a button.

Having such a Featured section is a double benefit for yourself and for your readers. You can easily point new connections or existing contacts in a direct message to a certain element in that list which they can easily find. And for anyone who is not your direct connection or doesn't follow you yet, this Featured section shows them what type of content they can expect from you.

As sharing content starts to become more important on your journey through this book, I highly recommend getting the Creator Mode, as the Featured section plays well with that different profile structure. Most readers follow some active content creators so they will automatically look at that very spot on your profile, too.

The saying, 'A picture tells a thousand words' is also valid for this section. The available real estate gives you two lines of text and an image in a wide landscape format which are both taken from the chosen items. Make sure your text and image look appealing to click on.

Here's how you use the Featured list to your advantage:

1. **Review** your best posts, checking whatever you published before choosing at least three of them. It's easy if you have a list with post URLs or use analytics tool ShieldApp (www.shieldapp.ai).

2. **Designate** those posts as 'Feature on top of profile' to make them accessible in that list. Be aware that the last item you add will be visible as the most prominent item in that section.

3. **Add** an external link to whatever you want to share, which can be a blog post, a landing page with an offer, even a YouTube video. Just make sure it comes with an image and a bit of text.

4. **Update** that list occasionally when you have something new to share. The idea is to use this as a shortcut to your best converting work, which advances your business agenda.

Once you have this section in place, your profile will look much stronger as an opinion maker, a content writer, and someone who has something to say which can be easily found. The Featured section plays an important role when finding out if we want to follow someone we don't know yet – or not.

☞ www.connectandactbook.com/featured

Details

Your profile is nearly ready, all the basics are included and some advanced topics like the Featured section and even the Creator Mode are in place. LinkedIn added a range of smaller features over time which make your profile stand out on the first view. Let's have a look at them one by one.

Let's start with your **Contact info** section: Did you check if the ways to reach you are still accurate? For anyone in customer facing roles I recommend adding your mobile phone number and email address, ideally a personal one instead of company email. If you are active on Twitter, you can share your handle as well. Add your birthday if you'd like to remind others to talk to you at least once per year. And don't forget to add or update your website.

The top part of your profile also has a couple of newer functions you should consider. Next to your name you can add your **pronouns** such as 'She/Her', 'He/Him' etc. if this way to identify yourself is typical in your industry. You might have seen the speaker icon next to the name as well. That symbol is called **name pronunciation** feature, a little voice snippet of your name for up to ten seconds. That is especially handy for those with rare names like me. You can also use this to add a bit about yourself like a micro pitch but it can only be recorded on the mobile app.

A recent and very useful addition is the clickable **website** link which is much faster and efficient than clicking through the Contact info section. The good thing: you can label it as you like (e.g. "Buy my new book here!") without the need to show the website address itself.

Have you seen that some profile photos have a circle around them? This is the **Cover Story** feature: a video up to 30 seconds showing a quick intro about yourself. This simulates how you would appear in a video meeting or face to face. It's a good idea to wear something similar to the profile photo and ideally ensure that the photo is not much older than the video. Like the name pronunciation, you need to add it on the mobile app.

The top part of your profile includes an invisible detail: your **industry**. You can edit that field next to the location info. LinkedIn enhanced the list recently. Most people forget adapting this when they change their jobs.

Have a look at the **profile URL** of the experts in this book. All of them show their real name in the link without the cryptic digits received by default. You find the place to change on the righthand side on the desktop version, just above the advertising box. If your real name is not available, please try some variations until you find the URL that works for you.

These are the steps to turn your profile from basic to magnetic:

1. **Enhance** the top part of your profile by recording your name, adding the Cover Story video and by including your website to appear as an approachable and genuine person.

2. **Fix** your profile URL and update the Contact info data to ensure your profile looks presentable when shared as a link in public. Make sure to include all that's needed to be reachable.

3. **Check** your industry info in the top part of your profile. It looks unimportant as it is not displayed but it is used to determine what type of content you see in your feed – and who sees yours.

4. **Add** another language version of your profile in case you want to address a market in another language. You can still decide which portions to translate but it will be appreciated by your readers.

Now your profile has all the ingredients to be quickly perceived as a magnetic profile showing the right elements, a story within the About section including your typical keywords and a range of newer features to stand out. With that in place, finding the right contacts for your network is the next step on our journey.

☞ www.connectandactbook.com/details

Digital Brand in Practice

Here are some further ideas from experts in my network.

Sue Parker
Communications, Career Brand Marketing & Job Search Strategist, DARE Group Australia (Melbourne)
www.linkedin.com/in/sueparkerdare

Trust and commercial ethics are a fluid concept yet critical for success. How people are perceived is central to reputations and perceptions are reality unless disproved. Rhetoric must meet truth. Any disconnect with truth damages personal brands insurmountably.

In this time of immense digital saturation and information manipulation, ethics and trust are the future of sustainability.

Depending on your industry, you may face considerable market distrust. Research from Roy Morgan in Australia and Edelman globally lists the most and least trusted professions. Although many sectors suffer poor reputations, there are real opportunities to stand out by demonstrating values and differences.

Competition in many sectors continues to escalate, meaning building market trust of your deliverables is essential. On top of that is the deluge of individuals striving for influencer status dishonestly. Content, media, direct and indirect relationships and social media form an integrity and ethics perception mosaic. All that glitters isn't always gold and discourages potential buyers.

Saying what you mean and doing what you say fortifies trust. Deceptive, unethical or disingenuous behaviour and services destroy it. In a world saturated with digital competition and copycat services, the true golden juice of differentiation is ethics and integrity.

Michele Gennoe
Mindset and Personal Branding Coach, Transformation
Specialist, Host of Mindset Michele TV Show (Sydney)
www.linkedin.com/in/michelegennoe

The children's story "The Emperor's New Clothes" by Hans Christian Andersen provides a good parable of the biggest problem for people when it comes to their personal brands.

In the story the Emperor wears more and more outrageous clothes and he constantly asks his subjects, 'How do I look?' Scared of offending him, people assure him that he looks magnificent. This goes on until the Emperor gets conned into wearing a custom tailored "special outfit" which is so special it's invisible. The people around him continue to tell him how great his outfit is and how wonderful he looks. Until an innocent child points out that he is naked.

This story is a good example about trusting the innocent and true part within yourself. Do not trust what the latest trend or fashion is on Instagram etc, as these are fleeting – like the Emperor's invisible clothes. What may be acceptable or trending today may become illegal or unfashionable tomorrow. What stands the test of time are your values and what you stand for. If what is popular aligns with your values then yes, promote it as a part of your brand. But just like the Emperor's clothes, don't do it purely to get the reinforcement that you are attractive.

In recent years some of the biggest brand failures in business were those where companies have claimed to be one thing and then deliberately done another (e.g., "safe" Volkswagen's deliberate emissions scandal, Uber's "bro" culture that led to the resignation of the CEO, Facebook's sneaky ongoing data collection of people using it).

True power and truly strong personal branding come from aligning what you present on the outside (your brand) with who you are on the inside. You are worth it, you are magnificent – present that to the world and let the world see you wearing the "best you" possible as your personal brand.

Olga Bondareva

*Co-Founder & CEO at ModumUp, personal branding and
Social Selling agency for B2B lead generation (Cheyenne)*

www.linkedin.com/in/olgabond

Social Selling is the systematic process of developing a personal profile on social media to attract customers, partners, or employees. Personal branding is an essential aspect of this process as it involves defining your positioning on social media.

This includes identifying the roles you want to broadcast to your audience, as well as the ideas, values, and aspects of your personality you are willing to share. Personal branding helps to build trust and establish relationships with potential customers and partners. Leads that come from well-developed profiles with interesting content are more likely to convert into deals.

When it comes to positioning, it's important for your profile not to resemble a company blog. To avoid this, I recommend dividing your content into three roles: Professional, Expert, and Personal. This will help potential customers and partners find common interests and start trusting you.

Luke Shepherd

*Senior Talent Acquisition Partner at Workday, Resilience Coach
and Adviser (Sydney)*

www.linkedin.com/in/lukewshepherd

Here is my take on builders vs. collectors:

The best strategy to build your network is quite simple in my opinion: don't have one. Instead, lead with value. Give, give, give… and then, you guessed it, give some more. The collector's mindset is all about me, me, me, and what I can get out of it for me?

A true networker is relationship focused, giving without the expectation of return, knowing the irony is that this generosity will come back one day in some form or another.

Summary

Congratulations, you made it through the first chapter. If you also paused and took action on many of the shared tips, your LinkedIn profile has definitely improved quite a lot. Well done!

Here are four key takeaways from this chapter:

LinkedIn became a global content platform like a stage with an audience where every participant can grab the microphone. Less than ten percent of those in the virtual room share their feedback about the performance. The opportunity to contribute and build a following is massive.

Leaders and professionals often care too much about their digital reputation instead of giving their stakeholders, employees or business partners a feeling of inclusion and belonging by being active on social media and caring about the topics and concerns of their tribe.

When you transition your profile away from a CV style towards a brand statement sharing your own values and drivers, you will more likely attract the desired audience and open more doors than you ever thought existed. People will get to know your work before contacting you; what a shortcut!

You can more easily earn the "know, like and trust" factor with a well-rounded, authentic profile showing the genuine person you are. Important factors like integrity and respecting ethical networking are visible in your digital footprint and the content you share or engage with.

Chapter 2

Connect

"Talent wins games, but teamwork and intelligence win championships."

Michael Jordan

The Networking Party

Imagine you want to attend a professional networking event alongside many people you don't know yet. Obviously, you would want to bring either business cards or some other means so that the newly met participants can reach out to you afterwards.

I don't insist on using business cards in the old-fashioned style despite seeing their power especially in situations where this is still typical despite the resistance to touching any materials after the pandemic. A classic example are the BNI (Business Network International) networking breakfasts.

You could also just show the QR code of your LinkedIn profile. You find it by clicking into the search bar on the mobile app, ask the other person to do the same and show their code, which you scan to send an invite.

Some more modern geeks use an NFC card which includes an embedded file that saves itself into the contacts (good luck finding again who that person was, as we don't always remember names, but hooks).

This chapter covers ten aspects of networking, both online and offline from the process of inviting and being invited so that you can find the relevant people later, going over finding the right composition of your network and building an inner circle, up to leaving a welcoming impression on a new network which then becomes your own tribe.

Many professionals attend networking events without preparation; they don't know how to read the room and leave uncomfortable that everyone wanted to sell something, when they didn't attend to buy in the first place.

You can change your understanding of both offline and online events into a happy networking party where people want to connect, are happy to meet again and can talk confidently about the progress of their agenda, knowing they don't have to sell directly.

The magic appears when you understand that **your network is your net worth** and learn how to find people behind your connections.

Interview with Wendy Lloyd Curley

Wendy is a master connector bringing people together towards reciprocal relationships in an authentic way. As an Executive Director of the BNI Sydney North-East region, she guides an expanding group of growing chapters. She created her own Strategic Networking Framework as a source for relevant business connections.

Her book "Stop Wasting Your Time Networking" is a practical reference for small business professionals and leaders who want to grow their business by meeting the right people with the right connections at the right time by using strategic networking.

Wendy Lloyd Curley

Founder and Director at Strategic Networking,
author of "Stop Wasting Your Time Networking" (Sydney)
www.linkedin.com/in/wendylloydcurley

How do you define Social Selling?

Such an interesting question. Usually it refers to using social media to generate sales. I've never really considered social media to be a selling tool, however, more a marketing and brand development tool.

In that context, Social Selling to me is about showcasing your expertise, demonstrating that you can alleviate pain points, promoting opportunities for participants, and telling stories about people who have successfully used your services.

Could you please share examples of successful business networking activities, both face to face and online?

I will use my personal experience to demonstrate the strategies I teach.

Chamber of Commerce events: I am a member of a few chambers, and I attend the monthly get-togethers. I selected those chambers based on their geographical location and the friendly vibe I got when I visited them. My goal when I attend any event is to make one good connection worth following up. Just one. That's all I can handle for follow-up, and when it's the right person, it's all I need.

An example of success? After meeting one person at a few Chamber events late last year, we have now met privately and are developing a collaboration that will grow both of our businesses. We've both written books, we've got the same target market, we offer different training, and we think alike. I wouldn't have met her without attending the Chamber.

Business Network International: The structure of BNI really was attractive to me as was the high touch model of weekly meetings and weekly participation between meetings. I have so many examples of success in this network that I will write a book about it one day. Let me share one of my favourite stories, though.

A few years ago, my BNI group had about eight IT professionals in it, in a variety of disciplines. My husband is also in IT, so I decided to invite the IT members to my house for dinner. I introduced my husband and then invited each person to share what they do and who they do it for. I knew my husband would be able to refer business to some of them because his target market was corporate and government, and his company was not a good fit for smaller companies who needed IT services. The result was that my family network could now easily introduce my network to new businesses.

Online Social Networks: I am a member of She's The Boss, a network for female founders. We meet fortnightly for an online lunch session. This group started in covid and continues to grow in the post-covid world. Why? Because of the quality of members, the consistency of the leader, and the power of follow-up. We collaborate on podcasts, meet in person when we can, and help each other market our services. I recommend this group to other professionals who I believe have the quality and influence that this group is known for.

I connect with all of them on LinkedIn and we develop the relationships from there. The abundance of business networking activities is one of the reasons I developed my Strategic Networking Framework. It's easy to do too much networking and not get results. One must be strategic in the evaluation and selection of the many opportunities. Time is money.

What are the challenges for professionals to find the right people while maximising word of mouth?

It's important to make connections with the right people and then to develop those relationships. A big challenge is being connected to people who can regularly and frequently recommend your services. Not everyone will be in contact with your target market or be in the situation where they can recommend you.

Who else serves your customers? Who serves them before you? Who collaborates with you? Who serves them after? Who competes with you? Knowing who these companies are and who works in them is the key.

Another challenge is expecting people to recommend you when you haven't yet developed any credibility or trust in the relationship. I know I said that time is money, but it takes an investment of time and effort to develop a business relationship strong enough for real benefits to begin to flow. Trust is the first step and trust takes time. The older I get, the longer it takes.

What is your top tip for networkers to open closed doors and create meaningful introductions in a sustainable way?

Have a connection strategy. What follow-up do you do when you have met the right person and need to start to develop that trust? My top tip is to document who you've met and what follow-up you like to do and (here's the real tip) schedule time after each event to do that follow-up. Literally, I book 30 minutes in my diary on the day after an event. Try that. I think it'll make a big, positive impact on your networking results.

Networking

Have you ever met someone for the first time in your life and believe you know the person already quite well? Welcome to the magic of networking online before finally meeting face to face.

If you meet a stranger at a networking event, you run your tested elevator pitch to them for an introduction. Or somebody else might introduce you, there's an exchanging of business cards and some small talk.

Here is a Social Selling example: Recently I met podcast host Darren Saul at a networking event in Sydney. He sat at the table behind me, and I didn't even know that he was there until he started speaking. I recognised his voice immediately. No wonder; I'd been following him on LinkedIn for a while.

That first meeting felt as if we'd known each other already for years. Well, we did but just on LinkedIn. We never had a 1:1 call but I attended his training and he saw my content despite never becoming clients. What a powerful way to build relationships online to continue offline in the real world!

Building the "know, like and trust" factor online is critical. LinkedIn can help with that thanks to some elements in the profile such as adding your voice and video to show the genuine person you truly are.

Some of you might think that we shouldn't connect with strangers on LinkedIn; it's even written in the Terms of Service. That is the same as attending a networking event with the organiser requesting that we don't listen to anyone or exchange any business cards. Simply doesn't work!

The advantage of LinkedIn over any other platform is the combination of professional profile information with the option of adding some proof points like recommendations together with content, to learn more about what keeps someone awake at night, to use jargon from the sales world.

That might not work for all industries as not everyone shares their pain points in public. For instance, a health or wellness professional won't be able to search for prospective customers talking about their body challenges.

The informed buyer researches potential solutions mostly online before asking suppliers or making decisions. The famous book "The Challenger Sale" by Matthew Dixon and Brent Adamson stated in 2011 that prospective buyers invite providers at the 57% point in their buying journey. I believe this has moved above the 80% mark since.

With so many online possibilities to research about potential solutions, it is important to build relationships with those who talk to the desired target audience. One of the best ways is referral marketing. Organisations like BNI provide a platform for that, or you can build your own referral network.

These are my recommended steps to build a genuine network:

1. **Connect** with suitable professionals for your network, beyond prospective and existing clients, also those who educate, entertain and inspire you.

2. **Build** good rapport with them online with direct messaging, commenting on their content and tapping into their networks, even connecting them with other people.

3. **Nurture** the established relationships based on genuine interest to build and strengthen the "know, like and trust" factor. That can include valuable insights on their posts or asking questions.

4. **Turn** the conversation offline either as a scheduled chat or as in my example, out of the blue and develop concrete ideas how you can help each other with a "givers gain" mindset.

Soon you will realise the power of connecting with people you never met in person before. From working in a local market with occasional visits to other regions, you are now acting in the global marketplace using the platform with unlimited possibilities – if we connect and act well!

☞ www.connectandactbook.com/networking

Invite

You've identified a person to invite to your network through an event, a piece of content or just from a list of people you noted down or remember – well done, now let's invite them. The easiest thing most people would do is to click on 'Invite' and receive that request in their 'My Network' tab. Easy. But is this the right approach? Probably not.

Please observe your own thought process when you receive a connection request. Do you know the person? Does the name ring a bell? Maybe in that very moment yes, but later?

When you want to invite someone, you should add a personalised note as a form of courtesy, showing respect to the other person. Explain why you want to connect and add a hook or two, otherwise it can feel as unwelcome as a cold call. Write that request based on them, not focusing too much on yourself and what you offer, like you would in a direct pitch.

Technically it is very easy on the desktop version to create that personalised invitation. You start by going to their profile, clicking on 'Connect' and a little window will appear saying, "You can add a note to personalise your invitation to X." Then you click on the 'Add a note' button, write up to 300 characters and you're done.

This seems to be trickier for the mobile version. Most people don't even see the three little dots (...) on the right-hand side from the blue 'Connect' or 'Follow' button. Clicking on those dots shows a menu of various functions such as 'Personalise invite', and from there it works like on the desktop version.

Sometimes there is another challenge on the desktop versions and mobile as well: the blue 'Connect' button is replaced by 'Follow'. There are two reasons for that: either the member switched the text of that blue button in their settings, or they use the Creator Mode which is built for the purpose of growing followers to engage with the content, not to increase connections.

Why would you spend time on a personalised invite when it technically works to just connect? The advantage is two-fold: you can search later based on the keywords from your initial message and you can demonstrate that the connection will be mutually valuable, increasing the likelihood they'll accept.

Some people say there's no need to send a personalised invite as it takes too much time. This is where templates are handy as long as you can access them from your smartphone on the fly instead of waiting until you sit in front of your desktop version. Google Docs are typically accessible from the cloud and placing them in a note taking program like Evernote is helpful, too.

These are my steps to invite others professionally into your network:

1. **Connect** on the desktop version by clicking on 'Add a note' and then write a quick message with searchable keywords highlighting why you know each other or should connect at all. Or –

2. **Click** on the mobile version on the three little dots to open the menu offering the same approach of adding a personalised note which will tell the other person why you want to connect.

3. **Start** a quick dialogue once they accept the invite to your network after you read their profile more in detail. You can add another hook based on something concrete they shared.

4. **Nurture** new connections over time by learning about them, by engaging with their content, asking concrete questions or expanding your network further into their connections.

This way you can build your network with a first impression based on building trust and respect instead of playing a numbers game. Plus, you lay the foundation for a searchable trigger sitting in the messaging section for many years to come.

☞ www.connectandactbook.com/invite

Connected

Now let's look at the other way around when you receive an invitation, with or without a personalised message. With some people it will be obvious to just accept them as you know them – right now. But be honest: would you still remember their name in five years? Maybe not.

I remember watching a video where Social Selling expert Mark McInnes went through a list of incoming requests to join his large network. He had clear rules in place, filtering only a small group of requests coming through. I'm glad that he accepted me; luckily enough I had met Mark often in person and was also connected with other suitable professionals to him.

When your network grows you might receive plenty of those requests per day. I suggest handling them in a batch process maybe once or twice per week as long there is no urgency, such as an invite while you're talking to them at an event. The batch approach has the advantage of focusing on the repeated task of checking and accepting.

Why do you need to check them out in the first place? Wouldn't it be much more efficient to accept anyone who wants to join your network? Of course not! You need to avoid allowing intruders to join your tribe. You are the gatekeeper for your established connections. Imagine a clever person from a call centre agency, who only wants to connect with you due to your large network. They can get one step closer to your valuable network and connect with them under the pretence of "We are both connected to X" – which is not a real connection.

Also think about spammers, scammers and bots sending impersonal connection requests just to grow and then pitch straight away. We don't want to have those in our network. For me it's fine to welcome people you didn't meet before, as long a connection can be mutually valuable. Some people have the word LION in their profile, the *LinkedIn Open Networker*. If you don't know that person, don't connect as they help others coming in.

Back to the batch approach: I open the profiles of all invitations with a right click in a new tab, so as not to lose the list, then I read every profile for a minute to get a fresh impression. Do they work in a similar field or geography? Who else do they know? Do they have a Featured section with content that resonates with my network or at least with my personal interests?

If they sent a personal invite: has this been crafted well so that I really want to establish a connection or is it too obvious what they want? After a while you'll get a feeling for those you want to add and those it's better to decline.

Once accepted, I typically send them a personalised reply, either written in that very moment or using a template. That message describes the hook of the connection which can be found at a later stage.

These are my steps to work through incoming invitations:

1. **Read** the invitation if they added one. Did they use a standard text or write something really personal such as, "Your latest post resonates with me" or "We both share an interest in X", etc.?

2. **Check** their profile. Easy if you know them, otherwise it's worth looking for something that sparks your interest. If you don't find a valid reason to connect, just reject the invite. Done.

3. **Welcome** them into your network with a personalised message. This will always stay between you in the messaging section. Find keywords, remembering the hook of your connection.

4. **Engage** with some of their content right away to show a genuine interest in building a relationship. Don't offer your services straight away, instead check in with them within a week or two.

Handled well, your new connections will become fond of your work and will truly appreciate you writing some personalised lines in the acceptance.

☞ www.connectandactbook.com/connected

Partners

What has driven me for two decades in the IT channel is building strong relationships with partner companies. That can be retailers selling to B2C or consumers, it can be commercial resellers selling to B2B, or any other form of partnership.

Partners also include consultants as well-known experts in their field and even established associations and renowned institutions with influence in their industry.

The holistic approach of finding and then engaging with suitable companies in between vendor and end customer is more than just selling. Partnership managed well is a two-way engagement, not just the journey of shipping products through a channel to the end customer.

I believe in lifelong learning, especially from those who are at the pulse of their end customers' challenges. I'm interested in those who are seasoned experts in their field who know all the relevant stakeholders.

I often call this business a triple-win approach – and when a distributor is involved, it can even be a quadruple win. It is just important to ensure that every one of those partiers can achieve their agenda. Even when changing companies, successfully built partnerships based on mutual interest remain for a long time when nurtured well.

Most business solutions are not created alone. Producing or reselling products and services usually requires business partners, resellers, consultants and many other kinds of supporting organisations. A true partnership means more for me than just calling them suppliers.

You may notice that sellers rarely promote the content ideas of their partners on LinkedIn, which for a me is a missed chance. Good leadership means also how well we help others to shine and succeed. As a prospective buyer I would like to understand how someone solves a problem combining several solutions together.

The challenge of supporting our partners on social media is often based on missing alignment on what you can share together in public. Especially for larger organisations it requires synchronising two sets of rules.

Imagine you are a selling a specialised IT solution. A future customer would like to understand how others solved that challenge, from decision and implementation to change management delivered by partners. The prospect would love to read about the holistic approach between all involved parties. But somebody needs to start and create that combined success story.

This is my approach for how to use Social Selling activities for your long-standing and new business partners:

1. **Research** the environment and expertise of the partner and their employees instead of finding the way selling through them. If you manage similar partners, compare their digital footprint.

2. **Connect** them with your network using a "givers gain" mindset to find out who could enrich their experience as a useful contact for them, both face to face and online.

3. **Share** ideas in a broader sense with the partner in open dialogue, knowing an end customer does not need just your product but will go through different stages, which means referring others.

4. **Keep** the contact alive even without current opportunities or when one of you moves on. A partnership is a village in its own right, not restricted to Sydney, Zürich or Vancouver.

Supporting your partners on LinkedIn encourages them to be more active as well which means enhanced networks on both sides, potential referrals and more mutual business. The word partnership includes *ship* because we are sailing in the same *boat* with common interests.

☞ www.connectandactbook.com/partners

Supporters

At this stage you should have your current clients and many prospective customers along with business partners in your LinkedIn network. Who else do you need to transform the dusty Rolodex from the good old days into a cheering tribe?

Let's check some other groups of people. Obviously you will have connected with most of your colleagues already. If your company has offices in other places or even countries, check if you or your team has one or more counterparts over there, as it's a good way to check how others in similar roles get LinkedIn working for them.

Please wish those colleagues who left the company good luck in their next organisation and find out if they go to an interesting place. Not everyone moves to a competitor; they might now work with one of those potential customers you had on your radar. It's often worth checking in with some of them to genuinely find out how they are.

The next interesting group are friends from high school or university. They might have started inspiring careers as well or now work at interesting companies, or perhaps they went in an academic direction. The bond from those earlier formative years can be very strong. I'm not talking about getting hired via old friends near their workplace, rather they might have an unexpected source of advice.

Studying computer science and now working in sales, I can call some of my friends from university who now work as CIOs at large organisations. Not to sell to them my products or services straight away but rather to get trusted feedback or to learn more about decision making.

Have a look at the business cards you brought back from various conferences or meetings. Did you ever follow up on those which weren't a potential customer on the first view? Most likely not. Adding them into your network can be a good idea as they can become your supporters as well.

I'm sure you've now found various sources for adding potential support- ers into your network. Obviously you want to ensure that those contacts from long ago or far away can still see what you are up to. Therefore it's a good idea to occasionally engage with their content as well. You could find out who from a sub-group such as your university contacts is also very active creating content on LinkedIn and engage with their material.

How do you deal with those former colleagues who are now your com- petitors? Should we disconnect from them? In my view, no. You can still be helpful to each other in a broader sense. One day they won't be your market competitor anymore but may be a partner or just a great former workmate.

This is my task list to turn real-life connections into supporters:

1. **Connect** with existing and former colleagues at work who are not in your LinkedIn network yet. Check who else they know to find out if there are mutual connections you didn't invite yet.

2. **Add** those from earlier times like high school, university, further educational topics, friends and anyone who could potentially be a supporter of your work – and cheer them as well.

3. **Interact** occasionally with their content or network, which trig- gers the algorithm to show your posts. Use the birthday reminders as your own mini prompter to check them out again.

4. **Connect** some of your supporters with each other or with one of your current contacts, as this brings value to them and you – that's a triple win!

Your network is your net worth. Building a set of supporters within your network is important to turn visitors to your profile into engaged fans of your content. And you have a broader sounding board at hand!

☞ www.connectandactbook.com/supporters

Circle

Your network is now growing consistently including those you know very well but also your new acquaintances or former co-workers from times gone by. How good would it be to categorise them a bit, at least into an inner circle vs. all others?

This task is elegantly solved in Facebook with the special list of hand-picked close friends. Instagram offers a group of favourites in addition to the same category of close friends as Facebook. Very handy if you want to share something only to those groups of people.

So far LinkedIn doesn't offer anything similar for all members. Only the Sales Navigator edition allows categorisation in various lists, both for people (Leads) and companies (Accounts). But we use this only for prospecting activities over there, not to group a whole network.

If you google classifying LinkedIn contacts, you might find earlier descriptions of the 'tag' field below a contact name which unfortunately was deleted from the platform in 2017.

It seems to me that removing that useful feature was on purpose, to sell more Sales Navigator licences. There you can sort a contact into one or more lists as a way to classify and group them easily.

Before looking for a potential solution, let's first find out why that feature would be great to have. If you want to scan your network for whatever reason such as finding a person in company X, all living in city Y or the second-grade contacts of Z, you can do that in the search bar by applying filters. Maybe that's why LinkedIn never found the need for a simple close circle group.

The main reason in my view as content creator is to have a list of people who might want to interact with your posts, either by commenting or you might want to tag them from the beginning. You also want to find out what your close connections are posting over anyone else. Like a shortlist of real-life business connections you can give a call when you need help or advice.

You can of course download all your data from the Settings within the Privacy tab and import them into a Google Sheet, Excel or any other tool for a further mark of your favour. But that won't be synchronised so it's not particularly efficient. Using external automation tools will risk your profile being flagged as most of them don't comply to the Terms of Service. There are legal and valid exceptions such as Octopus CRM but not for free.

For those who don't run Sales Navigator and prefer not to use external tools, I suggest a manual list so at least you have a memory hook at hand. This list will grow over time so the main challenge will be constant updating. Ideally you have a regular reminder in your calendar to maintain that list. What about introducing some of those on the list to each other?

Here are my suggestions to group your inner circle:

1. **Create** a simple Google Sheet or Excel with a list of professionals including their profile URL and email. Add a column for some keywords to ensure you can filter accordingly.

2. **Tag** a pre-filtered subset of this list for your posts or tag them in a comment as long you know they are likely to respond. Make sure you don't overwhelm their willingness to do you a favour.

3. **Set up** a LinkedIn messaging chat group if you want your inner circle to know each other. If you'd like this to be visible in public, you can also create an official LinkedIn group.

4. **Use** Sales Navigator or other approved tools if you want to invest in your tech stack or if serious prospecting is financially viable for your business.

Your inner circle of people will be happy as you interact with their material and network in a similar way to which they support yours.

☞ www.connectandactbook.com/circle

Introductions

While writing this chapter, I received a call from a contact I met in person a while ago. He saw my content over the last year and decided to simply reach out with a question about a problem. Nice way to move an engagement into an offline conversation.

The only challenge for me: I couldn't really help him by myself. I could train him on the topic but he was looking for an expert to deliver the service for him instead of learning how he could do that by himself.

Having a range of professionals for the requested service in my inner circle, I knew two of them could potentially help him. I asked further questions to find out which of those two would by the ideal one to connect with.

Then I contacted the chosen person of my inner circle and she had the chance to talk to him. You might say it was a regular referral situation which happens every day across the world based on a strong network. And you're totally right. Many organisations support referring others, either as a business model such as BNI, or there are even official referring partners in the IT channel who obtain a referral fee.

Instead of just calling the specialist and giving her the phone number of the potential customer, I ran the whole communication on LinkedIn. First I contacted her by direct message to check if she would be available to take on a new prospective client. I offered a phone call to share more details if she would agree to that.

Once she accepted the handover, I created a direct LinkedIn message to both, inviting them to respond. Once the connection was made, I left the three-way conversation to them. After a while I checked in with both of them to find out if the new connection had helped and if they got along well.

Like the artist who obtains applause after a theatre performance, I feel happy when I can connect two people from my network for a mutually beneficial collaboration.

The mentioned example was an inbound enquiry from a person with a need reaching out to me, triggered by my content. In many cases it works the other way around: you read about a person from your tribe sharing their challenge and then you come up with the idea of who could help.

Instead of the first person reaching out to you, the alternative way is you contacting them proactively mentioning their situation you read about on LinkedIn, another social media channel or an email newsletter you received from them, and then you would tell them that there is someone in your network who could help them with solving that problem or at least ask some questions to learn more about the background of their situation.

These are my steps to introduce people in my network for mutual benefit:

1. **Read** the posts of your connections not just for the content but also with the view of offering potential help via someone else in your own network. The post may or may not show a challenge.

2. **Chat** with the person who posted that triggering piece of content and ask about the problem, whether stated or if you read in between the lines, outlining potential help from your connections.

3. **Receive** a message or incoming call from the person in need of help, potentially based on your own content as trigger. Then ask them more about the problem, figuring out who can help.

4. **Connect** the person with the network member who could help in a mutual message after you've got the OK from the first person. Leave them to chat after the handover.

Your network will be happy when you connect them together with direct introductions helping them. And the more you help others with "givers gain" mentality, the more likely it will happen to you, too.

☞ www.connectandactbook.com/introductions

Consistency

Still less than two percent of all LinkedIn members are posting weekly content, either curated or self-created material, despite all the efforts of internal marketers or external trainers. That represents a huge chance to stand out quickly. It just requires one tricky element after getting started: applying consistency.

Before we talk about posting content regularly, another activity is required to be consistent as well: finding and connecting with the right people for your network. If we do that regularly, our network will grow steadily.

Attending Raul Kumar's coaching program following the principles in Jamie Shank's *Social Selling Mastery* book, I had to prove within a given time the four activities: Find, Educate, Engage, & Develop (FEED). This process taught me that finding people is a regular exercise beyond content.

I differentiate the required activities *for* the week and *during* the week, which reminds me of the LEGO® bricks mentioned at the beginning of the book. The part before the week is basically setting up the scene for the next couple of days, including elements of reflection and planning. A version of that on a quarterly base involves checking your profile and the strategic elements of your time on LinkedIn.

The activities during the week are more operative or tactical following your earlier defined metrics. If you decide to post once per day, you follow that pace. If you want to grow your network by 80 people per month or 20 per week, assuming a third will accept your invitation, then you would need to invite 60 per week, so an average of ten per day, assuming you work part-time on LinkedIn over the weekend.

The biggest challenge is getting into the rhythm of constant activities. We know this from other habits like grabbing a coffee or reading a newspaper. Therefore I suggest combining this into a daily ritual with a reward once done like a piece of chocolate or whatever you like.

Here is a tip I recently read somewhere on LinkedIn: If you start constant activities like half an hour of operative work on the platform in the morning before 10 am, then you will be surprised by how this feeling of achievement carries you well throughout the day.

Finding people as a one-off activity seems to be difficult, the same as writing a post for the first time or after a long break. Turn your desire into regular, constant action which later becomes a habit (as in my last name).

Be careful if that well-established routine turns into an obsession. Be mindful about the addictive side of social media (I admit that for myself). The world doesn't happen only online, and the most important conversations take place between people directly.

These are my steps to turn occasional activities into consistent action:

1. **Plan** your week ahead, prioritising the most important content to be published and the number of connections to be made. You can also compare results against your content calendar.

2. **Find** suitable professionals for your network, ideally from those who engage with your content or decided to follow you. Check who viewed your profile – a great indication of their interest.

3. **Post** your content during the week as planned or occasionally skip if you have nothing to say. Ideally you have prepared your calendar in advance which encourages action in a consistent flow.

4. **Review** your activities of the week against the targets set earlier and prepare corrective actions if needed. If you are ahead of your goals, allow yourself a little break, as long as you can restart again.

Getting started becomes easier with regular practice. This is no different to sporting activities or other ways to keep your body fit.

☞ www.connectandactbook.com/consistency

Templates

It is so easy to click on the 'Connect' button and wait for the other person to accept the invitation to your network. It is even easier if they accept it to overlook the connection between both of you, especially you can't quite remember who it was. For many it seems so difficult to send a personalised invitation that makes people click 'accept' and connect.

There is a little help for that situation by using templates for invitations. Ideally they should be adapted so that they don't read like a copy and paste. The obvious advantage is achieving the balance of efficiency with a personalised touch. So let's look at how we can learn that little shortcut. You will be surprised how quickly you will learn memorising those templates.

For my coaching clients I created a set of invitation templates covering a range of occasions to address those who viewed our profile, who commented on our post, those we met at whatever event (fill in the blanks for its name) and other triggers.

These templates require a quick adaption of the invitation process or a follow up afterwards by adding keywords which allow you to find them later again. The good thing: you can store those templates in the notes section of your smartphone, in Evernote, a Google Doc or a Word file for example.

Before the pandemic LinkedIn had a famous feature called 'Find nearby'. Facilitated by an event organiser or anyone in a group of people, everyone would switch on Bluetooth, start that function and LinkedIn would figure out who else was in the room. Many of them might be new contacts, others could be already first level connections.

The idea was to connect with as many as possible by just clicking on the button 'Connect' next to the name while the first words of the headline suggested a quick decision. Most likely 80% of the people in the room would then accept that – but obviously we have no clue who had actually joined our network as there was no time to build a relationship.

Typically I would follow up with new connections within 24 hours using a template like "Hi A, we met at the B event in C yesterday using the 'Find nearby' function. Just had a look at your profile and I see that you work at company D like my mate E / are connected to F / work in the industry G. It would be great to stay in touch." I rephrased the template for that event, watched everyone's profile and sent it with a few changes within minutes.

You can use templates also after a relationship has been built. Imagine you want to invite certain parts of your network to an occasion. Why not try using dedicated templates for LinkedIn instead of sending emails?

These are my steps to organize your messages with templates:

1. **Brainstorm** typical occasions for inviting others to your network which can range from physical meetings via those who viewed your profile up to concrete content-related triggers.

2. **Compose** a range of those templates for various reasons and store them in a place you can easily find again, both for working on the desktop and especially on mobile.

3. **Memorise** at least one of those prepared messages in your head to be able to send an ad-hoc invitation quickly when it seems to be hard to find the saved templates in that very moment.

4. **Write** a common message about a topic or occasion which can be sent to a range of people with only very few manual changes. This is more likely to receive a positive response than mass mailing.

I highly recommend using templates for sending and receiving invitations to build relationships. The aforementioned 'Find nearby' function has not returned, despite people mingling again in most parts of the world. At least it helped me to create a set of templates for you on the link below.

☞ www.connectandactbook.com/templates

Density

You know the question: are you looking for quantity *or* quality when it comes to finding people on LinkedIn or any other social media channel? In my view the question is wrong. Just change two letters and you get a totally different perspective.

It is not either/or. We need quantity *of* quality. If you just focus on many people in your network, they might be the wrong audience. Your content would not resonate, their comments would be short if any, and nothing comes out of it.

On the other side, if you slowly win the right type of people, your network will grow organically with content engagement and a level of caring for each other. If that approach takes too long, then the return on investment for being on social media seems to be negative given all the work without enough tangible return.

Therefore finding the golden middle route is the best approach. That way you will achieve the right density for your network. Let's do the math if you just see it as moving a numbers game along the funnel. Take this example: you add 1,000 people and get 5% interacting with your content while 2% of those consider a purchase. That is just one person!

The density approach, or quantity *of* quality ideal, toggles between attracting a large enough number of people in a pull approach, reacting and engaging with content with a decent follow-up to ensure you can filter possible leads out of those who engage. That concept requires ongoing content in a variety of forms instead of always sharing the same type of posts.

Companies are on social media for raising awareness of their brand and selling their products and services. Many professionals are on social media for building relationships with others and sharing content. The selling part is not in the forefront, rather in the back. People do business with people they know, like and trust. But do we have to collect contacts or followers?

The limit of 30,000 connections has not been changed over years while we can still have unlimited followers. What is the technical difference? Both can see your content and engage with it. But you can only write direct messages easily to your direct connections. The one-way approach of followers mostly prevents individual exchange unless you share the same group or they use their InMail credits to reach out.

Why would you want to follow someone instead of connecting? You can follow famous people like Richard Branson or if you just don't feel comfortable sending a connection request if you're not part of someone's circle but still want to see what they do, which also influences your feed.

These are my ideas to improve the density of your network:

1. **View** the profiles of your network regularly while asking yourself if they fit into the concept of density. Do they contribute or are they rather a placeholder?

2. **Invite** those to your network who only follow you but interact constantly with your content. Apparently they are open to learn more about you and build a deeper connection.

3. **Disconnect** from those you don't need in your network anymore. You can still follow them but they don't need to be a connection if you don't message them directly anyway.

4. **Enhance** your relationship with your inner circle by connecting them with others individually or adding a chat group to improve their social media activities as well.

When you focus on the right balance between quantity and quality, you will get more out of your time and effort invested on LinkedIn and social media in general. The same rule applies to the other platforms as well.

☞ www.connectandactbook.com/density

Connecting Properly in Practice

Here are some further ideas from experts in my network.

Peter Strohkorb

Founder and CEO Peter Strohkorb Sales Advisory, author of "Smarketing" and "The OneTEAM Method" (Sydney)
www.linkedin.com/in/peterstrohkorbsalesmarketing

Connection requests on LinkedIn have often been compared to dating. In fact, similar rules apply. There are two schools of thought on how to connect effectively: Quantity versus Quality.

The Quantity camp follows "the more, the merrier" method. Often, they use automation tools to send invitations to any number of users in the hope that a certain percentage will connect. For this group it's a numbers game. They tell me that the best way to ask for a connection is short and sharp. Rather than a long-winded explanation why it's a good idea to connect, they prefer just one sentence, requesting the connection. I find that the problem with this approach is two-fold: 1. You need to send large numbers of connection requests to be effective, and 2. You run the risk of offending the recipients due to the impersonal nature of your connection request.

The Quality camp, on the other hand, aims to connect in a more memorable way. We can group them into Endearers and Value Givers. The Endearers try to break the ice by finding something personal to say. That requires an upfront investment in time and effort, digging around the LinkedIn profile, reading posts, scanning their target's comments for something they can relate and refer to.

Unfortunately, there is no short cut here. Leading with something banal such as, "I noticed we have a number of contacts in common", will not get you there. You'll have to try harder to find that special thing you have in common to appeal to them from an interpersonal perspective.

The benefit of all that research and hard work is that they will remember you after they've agreed to connect with you. It will then be far easier for you to advance into a business conversation.

The Value Givers lead by offering some authoritative insight, a poignant perspective, or a (perhaps even controversial) point of view. They lead their engagement with something that entices the invitee into a response.

Coming from a perspective of thought leadership or subject matter expertise is a great way to start a conversation on LinkedIn, particularly when you are trying to reach senior executive decision makers. Why? Because they realise that there are things they don't know, but that they should know. They are happy to be informed by and connect with experts who know their stuff.

Shani Taylor
Mentor, Queen of Connection and author of
"From Ignored to Adored" (Sydney)
www.linktr.ee/shanitaylor1

Is your social media activity leaving you largely ignored? How often have you been so excited by what you've had to share and then when you check who engaged with you you've been disheartened by the lack of response and unsure why no one else saw the greatness of what you said?

The solution is very simple but often unpractised by most people in social media. Next time you go to do anything on social media, whether it is making a comment on someone's post, sending a direct message, or even sharing your own content, stop and ask yourself: *"How would I react in response to the comment I'm about to make or action I'm about to take?"* and if you wouldn't receive it well from someone then simply don't do it, share it or say it.

No one cares about you unless you can show them why they should in what's most meaningful to them – and what's most meaningful to them is: them. Master the art of connecting with your content and you'll create deep and rewarding connections.

Jane Jackson, *Career Coach, LinkedIn Top Voice 2020/2021, author of "Navigating Career Crossroads", finalist in The Australian Career Book Awards and Amazon bestseller (Sydney)*
www.linkedin.com/in/janejackson

LinkedIn offers a dynamic and vibrant professional community, yet many fail to capture its potential to develop valuable connections. Instead, they treat LinkedIn as a static online resumé, missing out on beneficial networking opportunities. It's simple to connect with other professionals on LinkedIn and establish authentic relationships. Regrettably, too many send generic connection requests without personalisation or context.

To make the most of LinkedIn, take a strategic and thoughtful approach to networking, find common ground and introduce yourself with a personalised approach. Mirror in-person interactions and take the time to establish rapport, demonstrate your genuine interest in building a professional connection. By doing so you will unlock the full potential of LinkedIn as a valuable tool for career professional and personal branding.

Damian Corbet
Storyteller & Executive Social Media at Storians,
Co-Author of "The Social SEO" (London)
www.linkedin.com/in/damiancorbet

What are meaningful connections? I see them simply as connections that are mutually beneficial. They may be potential clients or business partners. Or perhaps they are industry experts and thought leaders who add value to your life.

How do you create these connections? By listening, by talking, by engaging – and LinkedIn is perfect for this. It allows you to seek out and connect with people from all walks of life and professions – from all over the world. This has revolutionised networking. The secret is to add value. Share useful, interesting content and engage in conversations. It's that simple!

Summary

Now you've learned how to increase your network to welcome the ideal set of professionals instead of random strangers. We've also looked at the best ways to turn those into lasting relationships – good progress!

Here are four key takeaways from this chapter:

LinkedIn moved away from a Rolodex of your customers and workmates into a content-driven platform which allows many professionals to add their voices. Obviously, we want to attract those people in our field or area of interest and thus must learn how to connect and enhance connection.

Inviting someone into your network using a personalised invite is not only a question of respect. We should also reply when someone invites us. The personalised invitation has an excellent side effect when we place keywords, which help us to find the person again within our messages at a later stage.

Your network is your net worth built from many stakeholders. Beyond our existing and former colleagues as well as clients and prospects, we also include partners, supporters and influencers into our tribe. We can use like-minded communities to build an inner circle group as well.

Our network does not have to be extremely large to be successful. We need to ensure that the density of engaging connections and followers works for the content we share and the people who stand behind them. The second level connections often represent the ideal target audience.

Chapter 3

Content

"Content Marketing is a commitment,
not a campaign."

Jon Buscall

The Salt in the Soup

Once upon a time there were two small notification processes, used as a vehicle to transport a quick status message. These turned into massive disruptions in technology and human behaviour.

The first one was the SMS of mobile phones, initially to announce an incoming voicemail. The second one is the LinkedIn status message to share with the world what's going on (a bit like Twitter). The first became the advent of messaging tools like WhatsApp, Facebook Messenger, and Telegram. The other one transformed LinkedIn to become a content platform.

Ten years ago, LinkedIn acquired Pulse, back then a leading news reader and mobile content distribution platform. That was the starting point for LinkedIn to consider content as the future digital currency of the platform.

For many professionals like me, LinkedIn became a newspaper which we can shape and filter as we like. The Pulse publishing platform became the LinkedIn newsfeed adding the capability to write long articles, and then the status update became the post. Several newer formats like videos, polls or carousels have been added and features like LinkedIn Stories abandoned.

All those changes illustrate that content drives professionals to visit the platform regularly – obviously LinkedIn wants its members to stay instead of moving away using external sources linked into a post. For me, engaging with content is the salt in the soup; without that there is no reason to go to LinkedIn except looking for a specific person.

Getting started on writing our content or at least sharing something from others seems to be a massive challenge for most professionals; less than two percent of active members share their material regularly. Therefore this chapter covers my tips to learn writing confidence by finding your voice through commenting, then curating and composing your own material.

Getting started is easier than you think, so let's go!

Interview with Scott Rogerson

Organisations need content for their blogs, their company pages on their preferred social media channels and also for their employees. Successful Social Selling and Employee Advocacy programs also require robust change management and a content sourcing strategy.

During my partnership role at Hootsuite in Asia Pacific, I worked closely with Scott Rogerson, the CEO of UpContent. They add suitable content from various sources into workforce activation tools like Hootsuite Amplify to support social media teams and employees with ease of use.

Scott Rogerson
Founder & CEO of content curation SaaS platform UpContent (Pittsburgh)
www.linkedin.com/in/scottarogerson

How do you define Social Selling?

It is important to understand the difference between Social Selling and Employee Advocacy. While overlap exists, the objectives of each program are unique. Both activate the collective networking power and brand equity of an organisation's team (when designed and implemented properly) to progress the goals of both the company and the employee.

Employee Advocacy programs have matured quickly over the past few years. The objective of these programs is to showcase the merits of a brand or company – as well as the collective interests of the team across social media. These strategies grew in popularity as corporate marketing teams realized the potential reach that could be achieved when their employees distributed company messaging and thought leadership across their own personal social media profiles, rather than solely relying on corporate social media channels.

However, many of these programs quickly faltered as employees became more cognizant of the value that could be directly gained by having a strong social media following – requiring organisations to support the development of personal brands as consideration for these employees evangelizing the company messaging to attract customers, recruit talent, and build brand goodwill.

While Employee Advocacy programs can be valuable for all team members in an organisation, Social Selling programs are largely geared towards those who are primarily responsible for generating revenue. The objective of these Social Selling programs is to leverage someone's social media presence to reach clients and prospects in a credible way that stimulates engagement.

As effective Social Selling certainly provides positive equity to the company's overall brand, these programs are far more focused on elevating the individual as someone who is known, liked, and trusted.

Both strategies are not mutually exclusive and often the strongest Social Selling initiatives can be tangential to Employee Advocacy efforts and even leverage some of the same content – but there are unique differences in what should be shared in order to build a brand for developing a sales pipeline vs. espousing the merits of an organisation's vision, culture, and values.

Could you please share examples of successfully curated content pieces which led into sales or any other form of conversion?

First, let's define what curated content is. Similar to a museum curator, the act of curating content means to sift through a myriad of relevant articles, or other forms of content, that have been previously created and then to display these content pieces in such a way that they individually and collectively tell a story.

Each individual piece has merit by informing and/or entertaining the reader while the collection of works that have been curated allow each piece to inform how you interpret others and to learn more about the individual.

In this vein, the act of curating content as part of a Social Selling program is not a way to shortcut the effort needed for the strategy to be successful. Merely sharing content written by your firm will undoubtedly help me better understand your employer, but doesn't tell me anything about you, the seller, and the person I, the buyer, will likely need to collaborate with to get the results I hope to achieve.

There is no silver bullet content piece that will have your prospects fainting in front of your feet and begging to become customers, but by consistently and reliably sharing a mix of company-created and third-party curated thought leadership, third-party lifestyle, and the occasional promotional piece, your audience will not only grow, but become more active – keeping you at the forefront of their thoughts when they, or someone in their network, encounters a challenge that you can help solve.

Effective Social Selling isn't about over-optimising each post to please the LinkedIn algorithm. It's about being authentic. It's about building credibility with the right audience. It's about helping those potential prospects learn about you prior to speaking with you directly, so they know a conversation with you is worthwhile.

Taking actions that you know will allow more of the right individuals to see what you are sharing is important, but I would argue that it is more important that these individuals don't feel catfished when they get in front of you and realise that who you really are is not who you portray on LinkedIn. At that point you may have landed the meeting, but you lost the relationship.

What are the challenges for organisations to curate suitable and relevant content from trustworthy sources for their posts?

Providing the right content to share was the only challenge that most organisations were facing when Altimeter asked the question in a 2016 survey. From our vantage point, this challenge has only grown as those participating in these programs have become, and rightfully so, more demanding that the content they share truly reflects who they are and what they care about.

This often brings in the need to not only include content that reflects an organisation's service offerings but also the industries to whom they provide these services. For many organisations, particularly as their workforce has become more geographically dispersed, the need for content that reflects where they live and work is important.

Balancing these disparate interest areas while continuing to ensure the content delivered is valuable and also properly reflects company and (if applicable) industry guidelines can be a formidable challenge.

While much of what an organisation creates for the company brand can be repurposed for use in a Social Selling program, many of these same organisations do not historically have a function for curating content from third-party sources about the topics their team, and their team's social media network, would be interested in.

Too often the idea of curation is assigned to a public relations team or agency who is often well equipped to identify mentions of their organisation but whose tools are not helpful when looking for the most relevant information about an overall trend – and even worse when trying to narrow it down to a local region or geography.

Successful Social Selling programs recognise that, in many cases, the type of content that should be curated into their solution is already being identified by their sellers and subject matter experts.

These companies avoid the need to onboard a team to focus on content curation. They don't add a myriad of RSS feeds that overwhelm your sellers. Instead they're translating the filters these individuals use when reviewing content on their own into an automated system, and provide these sellers with a program that brings the articles they would have sought on their own directly to their fingertips and makes sharing them with their own network simple.

What is your top tip to mix curated vs. created content both for organisations and for individuals?

You nailed the top tip in your question. It has to be a mix. Whether your ideal mix is 50/50, 60/40, 40/60, or 70/30, what's important is that you have a mix of thought-leadership (50%), lifestyle (30%), and promotional (20%) content consistently being published to your LinkedIn profile.

In most cases, the thought-leadership part is a mix of company-created and third-party content. If it is in your DNA to create some of your own thought-leadership content, that's a bonus.

Lifestyle content tends to lean heavily on third-party material and includes pieces on your interests outside of work. Think of these as the topics that you'd be excited to discuss with a prospect when you find out you have shared interests. Charitable causes you support should also be represented in this content area.

Promotional content is just that. It is a critical aspect of your Social Selling content mix but shouldn't overwhelm your feed. These posts speak directly to your offerings and how you differentiate from others. They are conversion oriented and exist to provide an easy pathway for those you've built credibility with and now have a need for the solution you offer.

What differentiates this mix between a company and personal channels is that overweighting company-created content is better received when shared on company branded accounts than it is via personal channels. Why? Those who are following a corporate channel are doing so to see what the company is all about and thus naturally expect to hear more about their topics.

When following an individual, the same rule applies (they want to see what the person is all about), and thus it requires more than just company-created content to answer that question.

Commenting

In ancient times salt has been more valuable than gold. No wonder that the expression "salt in the soup" represents what really counts. Taking this analogy further to social media, the Social Seller is not keen about getting only impressions (formerly called views).

The art and science of using LinkedIn well – adding salt into the soup – is commenting on the posts of someone else and receiving them as well. While the word engagement means getting reactions (likes and the other emojis) as well, giving and receiving comments is what really counts.

For me commenting is still an underrated way to reach beyond your audience and to tap into the network of well-targeted others by using a carefully created and cleverly maintained personal brand.

As Richard Bliss pointed out in his insightful newsletter "Digital-First Leadership", commenting on LinkedIn spreads further than just the original post. Therefore we should pay attention to the impact of our comments.

Be careful as adding comments which are too short can backfire. If you only want to achieve a high number of comments in a given time, you might be tempted to just add brief words like "great post!" Other people might get the impression that you didn't read the post itself or can't craft proper sentences. This behaviour unfortunately looks like you don't really care.

It's better that you use commenting as a way to find your own voice. For many professionals it's the first step before creating own content when they didn't know what to post yet, while sitting in front of a blank screen. Giving your feedback on an existing post from others at least allows some kind of structure to express your own words. Sometimes LinkedIn even suggests transforming a longer, comprehensive comment into a post of its own.

Technically the reach of a post goes to a subset of your network to check if they see and engage with it before spreading further. The first 90 minutes count, therefore it is critical to respond to comments quickly.

I must raise a quick warning regarding engagement pods. These are free or even paid groups of people who share their content with the sole purpose of tricking the algorithm to get comments quickly. This is a triple negative game: the participants in such a group typically don't represent the target audience, their short comments are usually useless as they are missing a genuine interest in the other person – and LinkedIn would likely ban the profiles of these people to "LinkedIn jail" as they have violated the Terms of Service.

It's always best to use comments as a genuine way to provide further value, to add a provocative thought or to tag others into a discussion. Don't forget the goal of Social Selling: turning a conversation offline. There's no better place than starting with comments towards your target audience!

These are my recommended steps to learn the craft of commenting:

1. **Follow** content creators in addition to customers and prospects in your industry. Check their network size and some second level connections as examples of your target audience.

2. **Find** useful posts from those creators with remarkable engagement to see examples of how to write engaging posts, learn from them, and check how others add value in comments.

3. **Comment** in a thoughtful way by adding further insight from your experience for the audience of the original author and for yours. Don't just share their post to your audience though.

4. **Turn** some of your comments into your own content and then tag those initial writers inside your posts to build relationships with them and their audience.

If you want to see masters of commenting in action, I suggest following a selection of the experts interviewed throughout this book!

☞ www.connectandactbook.com/commenting

Curating

Finding your own voice on LinkedIn takes a while and requires regular practice. While clever commenting is the first approach to build a reputation, curating texts from external sources is the second step.

Using material from other authors is a valid strategy to learn the discipline of regular publishing without staring at a blank screen – as long you can tell your readers why clicking on that link makes sense in their context.

You might observe that most people share a post they found on LinkedIn or an external article without adding any commentary. Readers have to guess why it appears in their feed. Missed chance! We want to share well-curated material to receive engagement which we can later convert into conversations. That doesn't work if we only click on 'share' without any explanation.

There are many ways to curate and share what you learned from it with your network. I suggest starting with a holistic view. Assume your personal brand and a target audience are defined. The choice of content depends on your overall conversion strategy: do you need to work on the top of the funnel (gain engagement), the middle (nurturing) or the bottom (conversion)? Think about the emotions you want your readers to experience at the time of reading that post, e.g. refreshing motivation instead of boring finance articles on Monday morning.

When you are clear about your internal motivation for the next couple of months, add the external view. Are there any industry-related triggers worth mentioning such a new technology innovation like AI in mass adoption or is there a regular event which you want to use to add your view?

With that decided, you can research what external resources have published about the chosen topics and if the respective article hits the expected tone of your network. Always sharing links from the same sources isn't a good idea; why not toggle in between platforms like Medium or Thrive Global or other industry publications to provide choices and unexpected surprises.

Many gurus say that LinkedIn doesn't like links leading away from the platform, and using a third-party tool reduces the reach further. Following the steps below, curated posts can achieve brilliant engagement – and a tool like Hootsuite even allows you to change the photo of an external link.

Once I found a good article from the UK about receiving government support by adding home chargers for electrical vehicles. I wrote a summary including the right hashtags, tagged the author and few others, started with a question and closed with a clear call to action. As a result, this post received about 20 times the impressions vs. my followers with hundreds of reactions leading to many interesting conversations – despite the external link.

These are my steps about using articles from others:

1. **Define** the range of topics close to your professional brand. In my case it's IT support, software, partnerships, sales, Social Selling, leadership and personal development.

2. **Find** suitable content on reputable sources like Medium, Forbes, and Inc.com for your network. If your organisation has an Employee Advocacy program with a content service, even better.

3. **Write** enticing hook lines highlighting why that particular piece is important for your tribe instead of just sharing the post; this way you drive your readers' attention to you.

4. **Compose** the post about the shared content as if it was your own with a call to action at the end, tag the author and some potential others who are likely to engage with it.

Curating material from others is a perfect way to build up your writing experience and to receive engagement. After a while you will realise that you can easily write yourself, even without an external article in front of you.

☞ www.connectandactbook.com/curating

Creating

You've learned how to comment and add more professionals to your network. You've curated external material and become experienced in writing about the texts of others to gain comments. The next regular step is creating your own content in various formats. Just where should you start?

Creating your own content is the most personal method to turn reactions into conversations. But what to write about when you want to get started? Here is my own formula which ended up accidently having the acronym of the name of a well-known software for project management (no affiliation!):

- **T**rust: Write in a humble, non-bragging way, showing how you like to be perceived, building the "know, like and trust" factor.

- **R**esults: Share case studies about how your service helped your clients to achieve the desired transformation.

- **E**nthusiasm: Show why you love what you do with all your drive and passion for your industry, company, market and challenges.

- **L**earning: Report what you learned by acting as a co-learner, being a few steps ahead, rather than a know-it-all expert teacher.

- **L**ifestyle: Support others in your area or industry by telling stories of improving the greater good of the community.

- **O**pportunity: Finally you can talk about your concrete offering in a non-pitching style as well.

The main message here going along that sequence to choose your content: you should be able to share more than just one thing. Even as some gurus say you need to niche down – at the end of the day your network wants to see you also as a person and will happily engage with the genuine side of you. That includes occasionally personal stories where applicable. Readers will easily find out if you care or just share.

Whatever elements you choose for your content, your strategy should be executed with balance and relevance. Balance to ensure consistency and only what is relevant to the target readers.

Consider the right frequency in your creation strategy as well. If you need too long to create your own content, you surely don't want to burn out by overdoing the process. We don't post just for the sake of posting. And posting too often is counterproductive for reach and engagement.

These are my rhyming tips for creating your own material:

1. **Prepare** your content strategy which resonates with your target audience and suits their stages in the marketing funnel, from awareness to retention.

2. **Care** about their progress and transition in a humble way as an educator without pitching your products and services. Follow my method above or a similar set of steps that suits your case.

3. **Share** what you learned after attending events, conferences and webinars. Make sure to tag the initial presenters to start dialogues with them or tap into their audience.

4. **Compare** the improvements of your writing in style and impact resulting in more comments to engage with. Check also how your content helps others by asking in direct messages.

Now you have discovered the art of commenting, the magic of curating and the power of creating. You just need to define which formats are suitable to the stories you want to tell, which ingredients to use, such as hashtags, the sources for proper research, and the context your chosen material works with. Continue your journey on the next pages to master the transition from a static profile to a dynamic content driven engagement.

☞ www.connectandactbook.com/creating

Formats

Do your posts perform differently using various types of images or text only? Most LinkedIn posts appear in your feed with one photo, typically from three type of sources: stock photos, graphic images or real people.

The last option brings highest engagement as it shows the most authentic way. Marketing departments prefer the first two sources though – but this book is about posting from a personal profile instead of a company page.

Whatever image you use, LinkedIn shows just three lines of text with 'see more' at the end of the third line plus the image. Text only posts include five lines ending with 'see more'. The mobile version shows fewer lines each. By the way: Did you know that clicking 'see more' counts more than a 'like'? Many creators are using an alternative graphical approach by showing a text message in a visually appealing way, like in the form of a Twitter screenshot. This way they can show their key points without the need to click 'see more'.

LinkedIn offers a range of other post formats. The long-format article is good for SEO to build authority, but it is not popular anymore due to overall attention span reduction in users. Combining articles together, LinkedIn created the newsletter format to collect regular subscribers.

You can start a poll to request an opinion from your network with up to four options, running for one week. After this feature was introduced, everyone flooded the feeds with polls. Now it seems to have reduced, so using that feature occasionally is a good idea.

Videos became a massive hit a couple of years ago when it became possible to upload a native video, accompanied with a caption file to show the spoken text as well. Video posts build trust and get more engagement on LinkedIn according to Richard van der Blom's algorithm analysis. But not everyone is keen to appear in a video, either due to their own perfectionism or they don't want to show up in public. A tip to get started with video is using them first as an alternative way to send direct messages to people you know.

LinkedIn added new template options like celebrating an occasion such as a work anniversary or welcoming someone to a team, adding a new certification, and announcing that you are hiring or seeking an expert.

Want to create something more entertaining involving your network? There are three event formats available: LinkedIn Live, a LinkedIn Audio Event or just a link to an external event platform. To setup LinkedIn Live, a streaming service is required with a couple of choices to decide on. The Audio Event is LinkedIn's answer to Clubhouse. This is tricky as the process means we can only invite the whole network at once, not send individual invitations as Facebook allows.

Here are the most important format types for your posting journey:

1. **Focus** on the first three lines of your text to grab attention. You can include an empty line and add a question as a cliff-hanger. For text-only posts, add two more lines to guide your readers.

2. **Choose** real life photos whenever possible as they perform better compared to stock images or branding graphics and show the raw, unfiltered side of social media. Focus on output, not perfection.

3. **Start** a poll to engage your network by collecting feedback which you can later use to write a new post about the outcome. They have been overdone for a while so use them rarely.

4. **Create** an event for your webinar by just adding your link. Once published, your whole network will be notified without selecting. Attend Audio events to learn more about them.

Your content strategy should be based on a mix of various formats your audience is happy to interact with, plus some surprising alternatives to show your message within your broader personal brand.

☞ www.connectandactbook.com/formats

Carousels

The most engaging content format lately is called Documents, also known as carousels. The option to upload a PDF file was enabled in 2019 but became popular only recently due to the clever way content creators use this feature for telling visual stories.

Scrolling through your LinkedIn feed, you have surely seen the beautifully designed images, well suited for a smartphone display, used in a compelling way to show a message. Examples of those mastering the craft are the experts Ryan Musselman (hooks), Jasmin Alić (copywriting), Josue Valles (curation) and Simon Chappuzeau (strategy).

Can you adopt the same style, you might ask? It seems to be easier for those solopreneurs teaching LinkedIn. Corporate employees are typically not allowed to use their company brand colours, fonts, shapes and messaging without being called out by their marketing or compliance teams.

However, it is an opportunity for smaller companies to use this type of content format in a compelling way. Here is an example from Roger Christie of Propel about how the CEOs of the Australian ASX200 companies use social media (full carousel at the link on the next page).

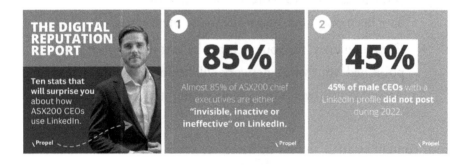

The best part? Carousels result in two to three times higher engagement than regular posts with one image, according to the LinkedIn Algorithm Research from Richard van der Blom and Richard Bliss in 2022.

Even when you don't have to follow corporate rules, it might seem hard to compete against what you see and thus you don't get started. It is easy to create a carousel in the Australian design software Canva by choosing one of their templates (see www.canva.com/linkedin-carousel/templates). If that sounds too complicated, you can even try PowerPoint.

Best practice from those mentioned content creators is sticking to the same design to be quickly recognised in the feed. As an example, I click automatically into any new carousel from Simon Chappuzeau in his chosen yellow colour because I liked his visual posts before. Smaller changes are welcome though to compare to the last visuals.

These are my tips to post your engaging carousels:

1. **Create** a PDF document with nice messages in either square or 5:4 formats as they work best on smartphones. Make sure that the first page has a strong message to entice the reader to swipe right.

2. **Add** a photo of yourself or a real person as in the example above to personalise your message over colourful brand carousels from corporations, which look like advertising.

3. **Write** a post with a magic introduction alongside your carousel which you add as a document. The first three lines and a strong message on the first carousel message will be a scroll stopper!

4. **Include** a call-to-action (CTA) on the last page which can also be a call-to-think or a link to a website. Make sure that the deck tells a story rather than pitches products or services.

Adding carousel posts occasionally with a proven visual appearance helps to increase your reach, followers and engagement. The personal brand as stated in your About section can be supported visually as well.

☞ www.connectandactbook.com/carousels

Hashtags

You know the feeling: you posted a great piece of content at the right time when your audience is awake using the right format which entices them to view, like or comment – but nothing happens. How come?

One of the reasons is missing the utilisation of hashtags. These keywords with # signs are used differently across social media channels. Do you remember the last Instagram post you liked? It probably had more hashtags than text. Instagram members often use hashtags to express feelings for the special moment, for example #thebestbookihaveeverread. Most of those hashtags have no relevance for searching the system though.

LinkedIn has a different approach: hashtags are mainly used to support the algorithm by showing your post to the respective audience. Typically they are added at the bottom of a post. Contrary to Instagram, a post with more than ten hashtags is classified by the system as spam which means limited reach. The ideal number has been reported as three to five hashtags per post.

The algorithm works with your behaviour: when you often engage on posts with certain hashtags (e.g. my own #socialsellingmonday), then it will show you more of other posts including the same hashtag. You can also follow hashtags to manifests which content appears in your feed.

There is another advantage to help the readers beyond the machine: The hashtags are displayed in bold and blue. Instead of just adding them to the bottom, you can declare portions of your text as a hashtag – as long as the words are searchable. As I write about Social Selling, I would rather mark that word within the text as #socialselling which jumps out at the reader.

Key question: how do you know which hashtags are followed by many people and thus enhances the reach of your content and fills your feed with more relevant material? Media expert and executive coach Sue Parker once created a book with the most relevant 600 hashtags, sorted by followers. Her regularly updated list is used by many companies including Hootsuite.

The search bar doesn't find hashtags easily. Instead I bookmarked www.linkedin.com/feed/hashtag/socialsellingmonday for my blogging series and adopt that for a concrete search. You can find all your followed hashtags on www.linkedin.com/mynetwork/network-manager/hashtags.

Can that principle really make a difference to the reach or turn our posts viral? Becoming viral simply means getting three times your followers. Once I shared a curated post about the influence of electrical vehicles on the building industry, added the hashtag #innovation (38 million followers) and apparently ticked many other boxes. The chosen hashtags contributed a lot to the 155,000+ impressions it received.

These are my suggestions to utilise hashtags properly:

1. **Add** three to five well-chosen hashtags at the bottom or within the text of your post, not more. LinkedIn is not Instagram to express feelings in a stream of spam.

2. **Consider** those hashtags which are logical keywords to be found for. LinkedIn's post URL includes them as you will see when you copy the link to your post.

3. **Write** some of those hashtags directly inside the post, not just at the end. This way you can emphasise a keyword to make a point by being blue and bold.

4. **Study** the hashtags used by visible content creators in your field or industry. Engage with those posts to improve your feed and follow those most relevant to you.

Using those hashtags wisely, you will see a more relevant experience when you scroll through your LinkedIn feed – and your readers will more likely find your content more regularly and thus engage more with it.

☞ www.connectandactbook.com/hashtags

Repurposing

Did you ever have a déjà vu moment on LinkedIn? You might have seen a post again which now makes sense in a new light. Or someone repurposed the material in a different context. What has been published can indeed be used again and again. You can call it reuse, repurpose, recycle – content can have new life in the original appearance or an updated form.

Adapting the posts is necessary though to keep them relevant. For example, most material published before the pandemic might not work anymore. And relevance to the target audience is critical to reach them by using the right keywords or hashtags and in an emotional connection.

A local example in my network is marketing expert Nick Bendel, the owner of his agency Hunter & Scribe. He created a range of videos on various topic in a timeless fashion that can be reused easily. He is better known for his series of having 500 lunches with strangers within five years. In between the posts of those lunch meetings he is reusing his marketing videos which now hit a much larger audience than initially. Keeping them in the same look and feel, he adds new videos as well. A clever mix of new and proven content!

A master in reusing earlier posts is content creator Justin Welsh. While not adding images to his posts, he often uses Twitter screenshots to visualise his message. Following him for many years, I recognised some of the older posts with marginal changes. Having a steadily growing audience, that particular post will surely be new for most readers.

Repurposing normally happens for a reason. Experts like Nick and Justin have a content calendar to plan out their posts in advance. If you want to talk about one particular topic, let's say you plan to contribute to an event as a speaker, then you might want to have a range of posts published around that event. You would surely write some ad-hoc posts to capture the live moment, but others can be indeed based on earlier publications, slightly adopted for the particular event.

You will recognise a range of benefits in reusing content. First it is faster than creating something new every day as adopting to a newer context doesn't take long. Another benefit is the learning aspect: when you look through earlier content to be reused, you will most likely recognise that your writing quality has improved over time. What a good sign! You may also be inspired to change the older material even more.

The downside is the requirement to setup a process to copy your post links to grab them again. Most LinkedIn members would rather go back in their posting history which takes time and doesn't offer any significant search capabilities. Better, therefore, to capture your own content regularly.

These are the steps for repurposing existing content:

1. **Track** your engaging posts by keeping their URL so that you can get back to them quickly. You can keep them in a Google Sheet or you can use an analytics tool like ShieldApp (www.shieldapp.ai).

2. **View** the chosen post with the eyes of your target audience: is that piece of content still valid and does it resonate with them right now at all? If so...

3. **Change** some of the words to adjust the meaning to the current sentiment to make it even more relevant. You might want to add a current addition or example to support the words.

4. **Park** the topic otherwise as the time might come for it to shine in a new light. You can still use portions of it in another context or just add this post into your content planner for later.

Remember that many readers will see the post for the first time even when shared again. Like in advertising, some messages need to be seen multiple times before they are recognised as desired.

☞ www.connectandactbook.com/repurposing

Research

Every now and then mankind moves ahead in a quantum leap with the advent of new technology. In a professional context that was the case with the world wide web, the smartphone, the various social media platforms and now with artificial intelligence increasing in everyday use.

Research for writing a post for social media has been straightforward in the past. We only had to check the links on the first or second page of a Google search and that was it. Many writers prefer researching distinct websites known in their industry such as the magazines Forbes and Inc.com, or they use blogging platforms like Medium to enhance their knowledge.

When the company OpenAI published their brilliant chatbot ChatGPT on 30 November 2022, most people didn't recognise that early how it would revolutionise the way we use AI and machine learning.

The first question on social media was the visible fear of it making content marketers obsolete. Many more people saw the danger in using the tool in a "CheatGPT" approach. Think about teachers who have to figure out which of their students actually wrote the submitted work by themselves.

We can also see this first mass adopted AI tool as a chance to radically change the way we search. Personally I still use Wikipedia as my favourite search engine, but ChatGPT quickly demoted Google to third place.

Now you might wonder why I prefer Wikipedia where everyone can change the facts without having an official standard like the old Britannica encyclopaedia. Google gives me only links to those websites who use reasonable search engine optimisation. Wikipedia provides me with useful articles about a topic with background and details to learn more where needed.

The free Generative Pre-trained Transformer (GPT) chatbot is based on a large language model of 175 billion parameters in the famous version 3.5 which provides conversational responses to the user's prompts. The available parameters used in the newer version GPT-4 reaches trillions.

The challenge in using ChatGPT for writing on social media successfully lies in creating useful prompts. The bot learns from the user and is patient when being asked to perform the same task with more and more details and in differently framed contexts over time.

Just copying the content from the bot represents a risk of plagiarism. While we can quote sentences from Wikipedia in a sense of "as seen on date X", this is impossible with ChatGPT as it would answer the same question differently depending on its learning from the user.

These are my steps to using ChatGPT for LinkedIn, well knowing that this is a most changeable and dynamic field at the moment:

1. **Research** your desired content as a clever shortcut compared to the infamous blank canvas, using various prompts to get different views on a topic.

2. **Prompt** the bot in 5-6 iterations to write a post and then craft your own to compare but don't just copy what the bot wrote. You can even import your own posts to teach it your writing style.

3. **Add** your own genuine way of writing with your personal style in a co-creation mode to avoid the content sounding like it's been written by a machine or another person.

4. **Learn** from other creators how they utilise ChatGPT to find your own approach. Some use AI tools like this one to update the About section in their profile, others only for their posts.

Using modern AI technology is a massive shift when applied well. As Raul Kumar from Resonate mentioned at a recent event, the use of ChatGPT and other AI tools can deliver a 24-month advantage over those who still wait on the sidelines elaborating on its disadvantages.

☞ www.connectandactbook.com/research

Scheduling

"Can I schedule my posts for the week like a set-and-forget approach?" I've heard that question often over the years and my answer remains the same:

"Yes, technically you can schedule your posts. But that is like a newspaper being delivered from the printer directly to the doorstep of your house. But it doesn't open the door to reach the reader easily."

That might be a surprising answer, especially as I worked at Hootsuite for some years, known as the first Social Media Management platform and the leading post scheduler.

There are a range of challenges to consider. Assuming we want to post so that people engage with it who we can convert, we need to post at the right time. A tool can help us with that – but it is not everything.

Since late 2022 it's been possible to schedule a post directly within LinkedIn without a third-party tool. That long-awaited function is very basic, missing a serious planning approach, a bit like Microsoft Word saving a file as a PDF. For a professional, the full Adobe Acrobat Pro provides so much more value than just the basic feature. That is the same for scheduling.

The real task is planning your content in a holistic way including organic and paid social media across multiple social media channels and comparing the relevant stats such as reach and conversion metrics with our earlier stated targets.

A successful social media strategy is based on a desirable return on investment (ROI) setting targets on engagement metrics. The experienced social media manager identifies the ideal time in the day to create a suitable schedule leading to that ROI.

Once the strategy is in place, we need to differentiate the process activities: planning, writing, publishing, engaging. Just scheduling even at the right time is not everything, regardless of the right tool. It is more important that our desired audience also engages with our content.

The best-practice approach across social media channels is warming up your profile by engaging with other active professionals before posting by ourselves – ideally with those who are likely to return that favour. The set-and-forget approach doesn't lead to engagement as the author wouldn't observe and react to their readers. Despite scheduling, we still need to be active.

The right tool uses AI. One example is HelloWoofy, an ideal platform for small businesses, who included AI long before ChatGPT. Hootsuite allows replacing photos of curated material, calculates the best time to publish, and introduced the new OwlyWriter AI to suggest and improve post content.

This is how you can schedule your content in a holistic approach:

1. **Create** a social media calendar with content format, frequency, timing, target social media channels, potential groups, and those people who should be involved.

2. **Write** the content in batches at once, combining curated work from your campaign and fully self-written material. Add ad-hoc content as well, aiming towards a suitable mix.

3. **Schedule** the posts by using a market leading software – I've used Hootsuite for many years, before and after my employment. It even suggests the best time to publish and analyses the success!

4. **Keep** active in the first 90 minutes after posting to respond to incoming comments, tag relevant professionals and share the post with a selected group of others seeking their engagement.

Combining pre-written content scheduled at the right time with real-life activity towards engagement reduces the stress of writing when you might not be in the right mood. And it gives you the luxury of planning and analysing in the same platform.

☞ www.connectandactbook.com/scheduling

Context

I am sure you've heard the famous quote *Content is King*. But be honest, what's king for you – content or context? And why does that question matter at all?

For me content is only a prince and not king when the material doesn't hit the target audience. What is useful for one person, full of perceived value, can be completely useless for others.

In my humble opinion, context is king because relevance turns data into information in the view of the reader. Imagine if you don't align the tone of your posts to your network; they will perceive your material out of context and thus refrain from engaging.

Where do the king and the prince reside, to follow the same analogy? In the castle, which for me means consistency. The well-established content creators Nicolas Cole and Justin Welsh taught me how to write regularly, and both are masters in that discipline.

Consistency is the combining key element to build a personal brand and gain business from the engagement on LinkedIn. Only regular activities bring rewarding results beyond a quick win or five-minutes of fame.

Here is a remarkable comparison between content and context from Erin Ashley Simon, posted as an article on Medium:

- **Content** is the material/matter/medium contained within the work that's available for the audience.
- **Context** is the positioning of the content, storyline or purpose that provides value to the audience.
- **Context** isn't just about the storyline; it is also about the intent of the content itself.

Our task as a content creator is framing the material to provide value to our audience, not just churning it out. The intent mentioned is the motivation behind everything which should match our personal brand.

This is a challenge especially when curating material from somewhere else. Just sharing a link to an external article won't be relevant to your tribe as they may not immediately see why you shared that piece of content with them.

Our context can change over time of course. To give my own example, I have been blogging about Social Selling since November 2018, first as a user to show others how this principle works and also for small businesses. That weekly blog and its associated online course supported my journey to join Hootsuite, where I continued to post every Monday about the same topic, the context evolving towards an educator. After joining the fine software vendor GoTo (formerly known as LogMeIn) I still crafted my weekly post, but in the role as practitioner with examples relevant to my workspace.

Here are some steps to keep you on track with context:

1. **Align** your profile to your values and the picture you want your audience to have of you, including the topics you share content about, even when you follow diverse interests online.

2. **Comment** on the work of others in context relevant to your own personality to attract like-minded people and potentially divert traffic to your own work.

3. **Create and curate** content in reasonable frequency to position yourself as an expert. Add the reason why you share that very piece including your learning for the benefit of your audience.

4. **Contact** selected followers based on their engagement regularly to turn conversions offline. Ensure that you also check their context over time by analysing their content for triggers.

If you apply the proper framing, the right audience will surely interact regularly with your material and are more likely to convert afterwards.

 www.connectandactbook.com/context

Insightful Content in Practice

Here are some further ideas from experts in my network.

 **Maggie Lower**
Chief Marketing Officer at Hootsuite, Pop Culture Enthusiast,
Music Lover, Board Member of Grindr (Chicago)
www.linkedin.com/in/maggiemlower

If you build it (authentically), followers/sales will come!

A good place to start with cultivating your own content strategy is to spend time reading (or "listening to" in social terms) content across the various platforms and see what attracts your time and attention. If your thumbs stop scrolling to read something, people in your network and those you might want to attract may stop their thumbs at similar content. It's a good insight; honour it.

You can amplify on social but being authentic, no matter what, is essential now more than ever. Consider exactly how much of your life you're willing to share to build your presence. To be clear, you have to be willing to trade in some personal currency or people will think you're a bot. Choose the stories and personal points of view that you want to share.

For me, I'm very intentional and thoughtful as I want to be the primary teller of my essential stories. You can still be effective online without revealing all facets of your life if you so choose, but I do think it's important to connect in an authentic way and if it's all clinical, it's going to be a slow crawl to gain followers.

Veronica Fernandez

Partner Account Manager at Aircall, championing the power of conversation (Sydney)

www.linkedin.com/in/veronicafernandez-wonder

Let's be realistic, creating content is not something that comes easily to everyone. At least not to me. But, like anything in life, it gets easier the more you practice and the more you do it.

When I decided I wanted to share my professional journey at Aircall, I made the commitment to post just once a week, not more, not less. Make it easy enough to stick to it!

Once you decide you want to start posting you need to accept that your content is not going to be everyone's cup of tea, and that's ok! You might also feel a bit awkward or hesitant, embrace it! With time, you'll gain confidence.

Where to start? Every week we share an experience, either something super funny at work, an eye-opening experience, or maybe we reach a new goal or find inspiration in a colleague.

I've found that sharing these are the best places to start. Don't be afraid to give a shout-out to a colleague or tell the whole world how much you love your job.

Tradeshows and events with partners or industry leaders also make for good content. Take a photo, post a video, write a few words, create a meme, dance it off. Make it yours, have fun, and share yourself wholeheartedly.

My second biggest tip would be: engage and comment. When you start engaging and commenting your brain will (unconsciously) gather ideas for new posts. Be curious, ask questions, start conversations! Often this will lead to the most insightful chats you will have.

Shuba Paheerathan

Partnership Manager APAC at JobAdder, SaaS and Social Selling advocate (Sydney)

www.linkedin.com/in/shuba-paheerathan

There are three components to how I create meaningful content:

Authenticity: The content voice has to come from you. Content could be a story from your own personal experience. Or, it could be commentary, a perspective on a recent trend. Whatever it is, it needs to be original to you.

Describe the why and the how. Content in form of comments, text posts or videos resonates when the reader can take something away from it. This might be why they need to care or how to take action.

Build relationships through your message. Any piece I create, I think of an actual person. It is not always the same person, but I definitely think, "Who am I writing this for?"

Simon Chappuzeau

Managing Director StoryLux, storytelling content creator implementing LinkedIn marketing systems (Cape Town)

www.linkedin.com/in/simon-chappuzeau

Your backstory is the story that you tell yourself and your audience about who you are, what you do, and most importantly, what backs you up on all of that. Have your backstory clear and your social media content will fall into place (almost automatically). Your backstory will guide you when picking topics because you know your sweet spot.

The million-dollar question now is: how do you develop your own backstory? How do you develop a backstory that's believable and supports what you stand for? A strong backstory helps your readers understand and trust you more. A strong backstory provides context about who you are. And a strong backstory gives you a clear True North on what to write about and what to avoid.

Summary

Well done, you've finished the juiciest chapter of the book, tasting the salt in the soup: working with content. As you start posting, more people will see your profile and you've learned how to connect with them.

Here are four key takeaways from this chapter:

The best way to find your own voice and get started showing your view on any topic is by commenting on the posts of others. Leaving comments with value, asking questions, adding provocative statements or connecting others all helps to increase your network.

Finding the right material for your networking with your own point of view starts with curating articles written by other authors. These curated works might be better placed than writing your own. But ensure that you add your magic introduction explaining why your audience should read it.

LinkedIn offers various formats to create your own posts with images or without, gain feedback as polls, get subscribers for your newsletter, show your genuine self in a video or use the highly engaging carousels to visualise your message.

Whatever method you select in your content strategy, make sure that you post at the right time when the right audience is not just in front of the platform but also in the mood to comment. That way you will gain more followers and drive more conversations.

Chapter 4

Convert

"The biggest problem in communication is the illusion that it has taken place."

George Bernard Shaw

Advance Your Agenda

Do you remember my definition of Social Selling as a clever approach of adding social media and digital tools to enhance business conversations? The target in my view is advancing your business agenda, whatever that means in your specific case.

At this stage our profile looks good, we've connected with the right target audience, we've learned how to comment on the content of others and started to publish our own material. So what should we do now?

Sending emails pitching your offers is not effective by itself, and on social media this is somewhat similar. Content helps to get a message in the mind of an audience but doing something tangible with it requires communicating with the respective person.

In a black and white approach marketing talks to an audience and sales talks to individuals. The content step of Social Selling has a marketing flavour while taking those conversations offline takes the sales approach.

Converting a conversation is the art and science to find the right balance between reaching out on social media and other tools to advance your own business agenda. If you want to sell, you can move your prospects along the funnel mentioned earlier. If you want to raise funds, it's time to show them where they can participate.

In all cases we need to learn how to communicate effectively here on LinkedIn and on other channels. It is not either or, we need to have a holistic view of communication channels in mind without being perceived as pushy.

In this chapter we look into finding our rhythm of content conversation, learning how to use messaging to stand out, talking to hidden communities and understanding the metrics to be effective. We also transition our offline engagements into the online world.

This last big chapter brings all the steps together and transforms learning into action. Applied well, you will convert your conversations!

Interview with Mark McInnes

Mark and I met at various occasions in Sydney, from the Sales Masterminds events with high class speakers to the Sales Enablement Society. Being known as one of Australia's early Social Selling experts, I had already put a lot of his advice into practice.

He uses Social Selling as a strategy within a mix of tuning instruments. Mark's insightful book *Tactical Pipeline Growth* helps sales professionals to strengthen their outbound muscles in the age of the informed buyer.

Mark McInnes

Founder of Sales Development as a Service, podcast host of "Best of Sales Skills", author of "Tactical Pipeline Growth" (Sydney)
www.linkedin.com/in/mark-mcinnes

How do you define Social Selling?

Social Selling is about meeting your clients and prospects where they are inside their fields of interest. This can be wherever they spend their digital time: Instagram, LinkedIn, Twitter, etc.

The concept is to build a level of familiarity through social interactions or engagements. This makes it easier for us to start, maintain and build on conversations. The more I see you in my feed, the more I like you and the easier it is for me to take the step to let you into to my circle of friends.

Could you please share examples how successful sellers embed Social Selling into their set of tools?

One of my favourite examples was Charlotte Lowry from Uber Eats in New York. When that business was busy trying to convince restaurants to come online with Uber she would reach out via Instagram. Usually through providing some interaction on their food pictures and commenting. Eventually, she would call them up and say, "Hey, I've been interacting with you on Instagram. Can I have a chat with you about your experiences with food delivery suppliers?"

Social Selling is way more than LinkedIn and most people get it wrong by sticking to that one platform. Successful social sellers are multi-channelling. They use social to find a trigger or to gain some familiarity and then move into a piece of conversation, usually in another channel, such as email or phone.

The worst social sellers are those who go all-in on LinkedIn and simply use that channel on its own to try and spam with an unwanted message. But social is not simply another spam channel. Too many miss this in their rush to 'scale' their outreach.

Ironically this scaling approach actually slows down their sales success. Instead, you need to slow down the interactions to speed up the results.

What are the challenges to align the typical elements of effective prospecting?

All forms of prospecting require some amount of interrupting. A call is an interruption, an unexpected cold email is an interruption, and an unwanted LinkedIn connection is an interruption.

The challenge for most sellers is their inability to acknowledge how this interruption makes most buyers feel and, as a result, they use the wrong techniques to try and push. Actually they use the techniques incorrectly.

For example, trying to convince someone to communicate with you by saying we have a lot of common connections is actually a good strategy. It's just done very poorly.

Here is the thing; if I think we are working, living or operating in the same sphere, then I probably want to have you in my network and I would be more likely to be happy to talk to you. So by drawing my attention to some others, who we know in common, is a good idea.

But that "Hi, we have connections in common" request is overdone and mostly performed poorly. If I said "Hey Gary, I see we are both connected to Gunnar Habitz. How do you know him? I'll bet he has also asked you out for a coffee at some point," Gary would much more likely to respond.

By making a more deliberate and specific approach, I am triggering a more powerful version of the 'Liking' persuasion strategy. Without the context or the ability to understand the psychology of how humans react when we interrupt them, most social interactions fall flat.

What is your top tip to convert conversations by advancing our business agenda?

My top tips are an amalgamation of the above.

1. Slow down your outreach to speed up your results.

2. Multi-channel: Don't just use social, it has the same effectiveness as bulk cold emailing. Very poor. Use your social interactions to provide the reason for you to reach out on another channel.

3. Understand the "Psychology of Influence" (Dr. Robert Cialdini) and how to use it to increase the chances people will say yes and decrease the chances people will say no.

Planning

"If you don't know where you are going any road will get you there." This statement from Lewis Carroll describes social media activities extremely well. So many professionals give it a try, don't get the – unspecified – desired results and then give up. Well, they failed at the planning stage.

You, however, now have a pretty good understanding of Social Selling with a range of practical tips. In order to implement the topic not just for yourself or as a dry run but instead for a whole team or organisation, you need to start with proper planning. We talked about strategic elements beforehand; now it all comes together.

Do you remember why you want to add Social Selling to the toolset of your activities? The target is advancing your business agenda with a defined target audience, which you can better prospect and nurture by adding social media into your repertoire of activities.

If your company starts a Social Selling program, these elements need to be carefully planned: clear program ownership with decision-making power, above that, the sponsorship on the top level of the organisation, aligned objectives with both sales and marketing, updated social media policies allowing employees to post accordingly, and of course a content strategy.

Just before becoming obsessed with Social Selling myself, I was involved in a program at an earlier company. Despite an expert from LinkedIn supporting the trial, the program was abandoned as it was missing the sponsorship and management alignment from the top.

Later I designed a program by myself to get teams started, like a pilot program. Using gamification in a 30-day challenge, I see members of that program still using Social Selling actively as part of their habits.

Proper planning requires having relevant analytics in place. Please refer to the Metrics section in this chapter which provides a list of tools you can use to compare and adjust accordingly.

Beyond the holistic planning exercise you will also run weekly planning. The first part of that is the plan *for* the week:

- **Educate**: Plan and write content in batches
- **Enjoy**: Learn for your personal growth
- **Examine**: Review what worked, adjust where needed

The second plan *during* the week covers daily activities of about 30 min on LinkedIn without wasting time. It includes these steps:

- **Establish**: Build connections with those who viewed you
- **Engage**: Nurture your contacts and comment on their posts
- **Evolve**: Advance discussions in direct messages towards offline

These are my planning steps for your Social Selling activities:

1. **Define** your strategy including relevant metrics (see below) and targets. You might want to engage an expert to run an audit on what you already have in place and what is still missing.

2. **Create** a content strategy with curated and self-written material that attracts the desired audience. Parts of that will be placed on social media, others on your blog or appear in other formats.

3. **Execute** on the strategy with consistent activities on a daily base to ensure your content converts along the funnel in the view of the buying journey of your prospects.

4. **Measure** success regularly to check the results compared to your plan. Talk to the target audience when something works very well or doesn't resonate at all. Loop back to improve that.

A well-planned strategy executed well overperforms occasionally created posts without knowing the reason for their success. Best to include others in the process – Social Selling is a team sport!

☞ www.connectandactbook.com/planning

Messaging

Have you already overlooked messages received on LinkedIn? Most likely you don't treat the messaging section with the same priority as your email inbox. No wonder, as that function used to be far too basic for serious conversations. Time to have a look again after recent changes.

You know the dilemma: you exchanged ideas with somebody and were about to turn the conversation into an exchange by email to arrange details for a meeting. But where did that message go? All those birthday wishes, work anniversary congratulations and other less relevant notes filled your LinkedIn inbox so you didn't find what really mattered. Out of sight, out of mind. With it, your best chances for a meeting with your prospect – gone.

If we want to advance our Social Selling activities, LinkedIn messaging is an important place with surprising ways to disrupt your prospects, so it's time to get familiar with it. Did you ever send a voice message on LinkedIn? If not, it is very similar to WhatsApp or Facebook Messenger. Let me assume you also haven't shared a video message yet? Both are surprising ways to send a message in an unexpected way showing the genuine person you are instead of any pre-produced template, a virtual assistant or even AI sending messages.

Imagine someone likes your post, a person close to your target persona but not a decision maker. You recognise they might be a good contact to the relevant stakeholders in their organisation. Would you ask them straight away for the best person? Surely not. Instead, use LinkedIn as a messaging tool to build a relationship with them. Once the rapport is built, connect with them and also engage on their material and of their colleagues.

When the time is right, you can ask: "Do you think that Caroline or David might benefit from that post as well?" Thus showing that you researched their organisation which underlines your commitment and familiarity with their industry. Then it is just a matter of time to schedule a phone call or video conference with the initial person or even several at once.

You can also use LinkedIn messages as a search engine. Imagine you attend an event, connect with many people at once but don't remember all their names. When you include a hook in your personalised invite or in your follow up message, you can search for the keywords placed there and find who that person was. That can lead to engaging in further conversations with them.

Quick warning at this stage: don't use LinkedIn automation tools, even when they promise to enhance the experience by mass messaging or inviting your prospects automatically. First of all, it is against the Terms of Service and you risk being banned. Moreover, your connections will sense by the tone in the message that it doesn't come directly from you which destroys their trust.

These are my suggestions for mastering LinkedIn messaging:

1. **Check** your messages daily supporting the expectation of instant messaging. Respond professionally using emojis where applicable. Cultivate a conversation before offering anything too quickly.

2. **Record** voice and video messages for individual recipients only in the mobile app which has the respective buttons at the bottom. For voice messages hold for 60 seconds, videos run for two mins.

3. **Organise** your inbox by marking important conversations with a star like in Gmail, keeping those relevant in the 'Focused' section, moving less relevant into 'Other' and archive the rest.

4. **Learn** additional features like editing a message after being sent, forwarding a message to another person, and prepare for a leave period with an 'Away message' reply.

Now you know how to complete the full circle from having a magnetic profile via connecting with impact and using converting content, up to exchanging messages to advance a conversation.

☞ www.connectandactbook.com/messaging

Cadence

You now know how to handle LinkedIn from branding to content. You have learned how to message towards conversion which means advancing your business agenda. Your experience tells you that LinkedIn is not everything and many people want to be reached on more than one channel.

As Mark McInnes pointed out in his book *Tactical Pipeline Growth*, "Don't be a desperate seller. Nothing smells worse than commission breath." We need to find a clever way to turn readers into prospective buyers at the different stages in the funnel.

Timing is important in Social Selling – you don't want to pitch when the prospect is not ready to buy. You also don't want to just inform for awareness and miss out as it wasn't clear to your future client how to book you.

Mark introduced the concept of a cadence in his book, describing "a series of touches strategically placed across multiple communication channels over a defined period. When consistently and patiently applied, it dramatically increases prospect reply rates and lead qualification."

Those of us in a professional sales role know the concept of sending a series of emails in a defined or ad-hoc frequency to educate and add a call-to-action, often the same request across the sequence. Email automation tools support this approach and report to sales management about their efficiency. That numbers game method, however, often ignores the importance of grabbing the prospects at the right stage within their own buying journey.

A cadence works differently, covering a range of steps which Mark defined as touch points, channels, attempts, duration, frequency, and content. While we have already covered the last step, the rest may be new for many.

Imagine you have a new solution you want to promote to a dedicated niche of prospective buyers. Instead of just posting about it every day covering the frequency and content aspect, you want to build a whole campaign in the form of a cadence to predict results.

This is the example of an eight-week cadence, taken from Mark's book *Tactical Pipeline Growth*.

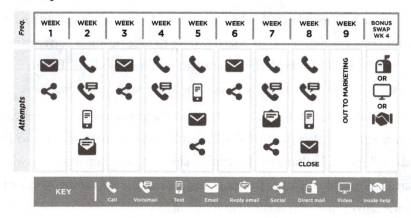

These are my ideas about starting your own:

1. **Define** the strategic components of the cadence such as the target audience, their preferred channels, the possible duration with the required frequency, and the content also outside of social media.

2. **Prepare** the individual touch points to set the tone well. Ask those you know in the targeted audience if your planned style and frequency hit the mark.

3. **Feed** the tech stack like your CRM system with contact details and all you need to know about your prospects. Add numbers in your phone to recognise them along their funnel journey.

4. **Run** the cadence with the required discipline by the defined steps and add new prospects every week like a well-oiled machine. Adjust the process as you work in a constant improvement loop.

Starting a cadence across multiple channels with Social Selling at the heart might take a while but will result in highly targeted engagement from the desired audience to advance your business agenda – which is to help them to achieve theirs, which in turn helps yours.

☞ www.connectandactbook.com/cadence

Offline

My favourite formula on LinkedIn is called Offline-Online-Offline. Remembering my definition of Social Selling to take business conversations to the next level, this typically means from online to offline. But in many cases a conversation actually starts offline at the very beginning.

Especially since most of us are back after the pandemic in whatever form of physical workplace possibilities, refreshing our connections face to face feels really good! In that sense LinkedIn helps nurturing conversations which started in real life earlier – to bring them back into the offline world with phone calls or meetings at the right moment.

One of my favourite stories about this formula goes back to 2018 when I attended a partner event of the Australian Reseller Network (ARN). At my table I talked to various people, especially those extroverts who enjoy speaking with strangers. A more silent fellow had a lot of expertise in my area of business but didn't share too much in that initial round. Let's call him John.

At the end of the event we exchanged our business cards which often means nothing if nobody follows up afterwards. I don't remember who made the first contact, but we met eventually for a coffee. We didn't close any business as the moment wasn't right.

About a year later John listened to one of my few appearances on a local radio station (today I would call it podcast) and rang me on the following day. Within one week we signed an agreement. How did that happen?

During that year John and I engaged regularly on our content on LinkedIn. This felt natural, both being interested in the same field of interest around Cloud Backup and Disaster Recovery (highly specialised for some and boring for others).

The conversation only needed a trigger for one of us to move from classic nurturing into the readiness of purchasing concrete services. As we'd gained mutual trust via LinkedIn since we met, I became his supplier of choice.

This true story from offline to online and back offline went on for a year of occasional engagement either on social media or even over the phone. And I have experienced numerous examples proving this formula works well.

The challenge of this approach comes in a range of aspects: First of all we need to recognise at the beginning if an acquaintance is worth nurturing. Then we need to keep them on our radar to ensure we don't forget them.

LinkedIn does not offer any help for grouping contacts, only the Sales Navigator edition has this option to categorise people and add searchable notes. And then we still need to find the right trigger.

Here's how you can leverage the moving engagement between offline and online and back again to nurture your contacts towards conversion:

1. **Build** good rapport with those you met face to face and connect with a personalised invite so that the initial conversation stays in the messages. Good idea to use keywords to find it easily.

2. **Reach out** to the person online by sharing educational tips or by asking them questions in direct messages without the classic pitch. They are not ready to buy, neither are you.

3. **Nurture** the established relationship based on genuine interest into their line of business, their industry and network to build the "know, like and trust" factor.

4. **Turn** the conversation offline again into a phone call, a coffee meeting or on video at a certain trigger presenting concrete ideas how you can help them to advance their business agenda.

You will be surprised that the transition between the initial offline meeting and a current face to face gathering meeting feels like talking to a business friend who you know very well!

☞ www.connectandactbook.com/offline

Communities

What is the difference between Facebook groups and LinkedIn groups? My provocative answer: the first one feels like a party, the latter rather like a cemetery.

They share mutual concepts: creating a closed user group with an outer guard before admitting future members to ensure the desired set of people comes together to discuss topics hidden from the general public.

The advantage of this concept: members can communicate between each other directly without the need to become a friend or direct connection. The disadvantage for both channels: groups are living (and dying) due to the regular or missing activities of the group leaders.

There is another advantage which most members don't utilise – people joined groups according to their industry or profession many years ago but most of them never left, even when the group became passive. We can still use that to enlarge our network.

Imagine you are a Risk Management Consultant keen to find like-minded professionals or decision makers in that field. You would join groups of different disciplines such as Emergency Management, Operative Security or Business Continuity. The admins of those groups might not run regular activities but occasionally accept new members. Once you joined those groups, you have full access to the other members.

Obviously we shouldn't misuse the freshly granted access to group members for pitching efforts. But it's a great chance to see who else hangs out there, what they share, and which organisations they represent or work with. A perfect place to find prospects, partners or supporters for your own business and for your network. And you can be a member of 100 groups.

In that sense LinkedIn groups might look like a cemetery from the outside but are very useful once you're in the club. If the community is actively discussing topics where you can add your point of view, it gets even better.

Do you know how many groups list you as a member? You can find them in the LinkedIn homepage on the bottom left. A faster way is going to www.linkedin.com/groups to see your groups and those you requested access to.

There is another way to create a smaller closed community in the form of a chat group. Go to the Messaging section and create a fresh message to several people at once, naming that conversation. All members can now contribute to the discussion equally and add others without the need for an admin. The chat group can be easily found in the Messaging tab within all the other conversations. It falls further down the list when nobody contributes.

This is how you can utilise the power of LinkedIn communities to find relevant professionals and get more eyes on your content:

1. **Search** suitable groups by typing a keyword in the search bar and then clicking on 'Groups' below that search bar to receive a list of groups with short descriptions (sorted without logical order).

2. **Open** some of those groups with a right click into a separate tab browser to go through them separately without losing your results list (this works better on the desktop version than on mobile).

3. **Join** the desired groups and contact their admin if not accepted or if you have any questions. Best practice is to follow those who lead the group and engage with their content.

4. **Engage** with content and members in an ethical way by adding value, asking good questions and showing that you are willing to contribute to the conversations (without pitching your stuff).

You will welcome more relevant contacts on a global landscape into your tribe and build relationships you would otherwise not be able to find. Plus the good thing is that you can create your own group as well!

☞ www.connectandactbook.com/communities

Advanced

Every topic we've touched so far in this book is based on the free version of LinkedIn without paying any further subscription. We've kept advertising and the recruiter edition outside of our scope. Here are three areas where you can enrich your Social Selling journey which you should know about and consider joining where applicable.

The first is the **Premium** edition which allows you enhance your search attempts without notifications that you've exceeded your limits. There is more than one edition available, in my view the most useful is the Premium Career version, even when you're not looking for job changes.

The main advantage is the visibility of those who viewed your profile over the last 90 days instead of just the last five people as in the free version. Whoever lands on your profile might be keen to learn more about you, your content and your network. But without knowing who that was, you can't reach out to them. You also get five InMail credits per month to write direct messages to people you're not connected with. If they respond, you get that one back. The Premium Business option costs typically 50% more than Premium Career just for getting 15 InMail credits and other company insights.

Is a Premium subscription worth the money? Certainly, if you use the first 30 days for free as a test and use the time to research those profile views with discipline and consistency. You will get faster to your ultimate target as social seller: advancing your business agenda.

Sales professionals in particular should use the **Sales Navigator** edition, available for individuals, teams and Enterprise customers. I tested all three of them and would not want to live without it. Key advantages for me are detailed search capabilities of leads (people) and accounts (companies) with the chance to save searches, categories and notes about them. My Sales Navigator feed is built purely about those I follow, telling me exactly what they post, who joined those companies, when people move, etc.

LinkedIn Sales Navigator comes with its own KPI Social Selling Index (SSI) consisting of four metrics: personal brand, search people, engage with insights and build relationships in a range of up to 100 points. You can access yours on www.linkedin.com/sales/ssi even without having a paid subscription.

How do you know what to write without listening to your audience first? The third advanced element is **Social Listening**. Here you track your social media channels for mentions of your brand or key staff members as well as relevant keywords and hashtags. There are various ways, from a simple saved Google search or Twitter list, right up to intelligence tools such as Talkwalker.

These are my tips to enhance your LinkedIn experience with paid subscriptions for enhanced Social Selling activities:

1. **Check** who viewed your profile using the Premium edition and turn those viewers into followers and connections, then to raving fans and repeat clients.

2. **Message** people you're not connected to using the InMail credits per month within the Premium edition. The better you target, the more likely they will respond and you get your credits back.

3. **Search** and store the results in Sales Navigator for serious sales professionals leveraging the best LinkedIn has to offer including a much more relevant newsfeed and insight about the right people.

4. **Listen** to your brand, keywords, hashtags and topics in a Social Listening platform. Start with Google and Twitter for free or use external tools paid for by your company.

Using advanced (paid) services, you enhance your search requirements into a highly targeted niche of prospects for your Social Selling activities, resulting in an increased outcome, faster.

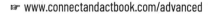 ☞ www.connectandactbook.com/advanced

Metrics

We use Social Selling activities to advance our business agenda. But what does that actually mean? How can you measure this advancement from the top to the bottom of the funnel, to use modern marketing jargon?

Compared to the funnel on a cruise ship, the marketing funnel goes the other way around, from a lot of people at the top to less at the bottom. The famous model AIDA (Attention, Interest, Desire, Action) was coined in 1921. For digital marketing I prefer Dave Chaffey's acronym RACE:

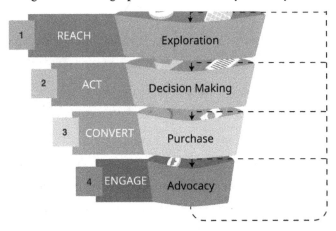

(found on www.growth-hackers.net/top-marketing-models-need-to-know-digital-model-framework)

Adding another simplification: the top of the funnel is about marketing (talking to an audience), the middle of the funnel is a nurturing process (interested but not yet ready to buy) while leading towards the bottom of the funnel is a sales activity (talking to an individual). Advocacy represents the transition from customers to raving, recommending fans.

The relevant social media metrics at the top of the funnel are the number of followers as potential reach, the views or impressions of a post, its reactions (likes and the other symbols) and finally the comments. Many gurus recommend ignoring the views. But in my humble opinion there are no comments without likes and no likes without views. Nobody would see content without a decent following.

In the middle of the funnel we see a mix of public posts with a nurturing character and direct messages to check in with them by providing further value. Don't just ask them for the sale at this stage! Finally at the bottom of the funnel we can measure our activities with revenue, profit or however we review our business target achievements.

The key for every social media marketing manager is first to understand and then to drive a positive Return on Investment (ROI). It requires having the relevant metrics in place. LinkedIn's Social Selling Index as mentioned earlier only shows how well a member complies to their algorithm.

These are my recommendations to measure your metrics which help you to adopt your activities accordingly:

1. **Learn** about the various metrics on the Hootsuite blog using the link https://blog.hootsuite.com/social-media-metrics which covers KPIs like conversation rate or social share of voice as well.

2. **Upgrade** to LinkedIn Premium to see who viewed your profile over the last 90 days as an invaluable list for reaching out to those professionals, thus directing them further through the funnel.

3. **Subscribe** to ShieldApp (www.shieldapp.ai) to get detailed analytics about your posts over the years comparing performance and reach. It also lists all your posts with links to repurpose them.

4. **Reverse** the calculation approach by setting smart goals with a conversion target to achieve the required top of the funnel metrics which help you to craft your posts accordingly.

By measuring your activities, finetuning the approach and reacting where needed you can reach your goals much faster than just by posting with focus on views, likes and comments.

☞ www.connectandactbook.com/metrics

Hook

No hook, no look – imagine you found great content for your network on LinkedIn, you pressed 'share' but nothing happens. No reaction, nobody seems to take notice at all.

There might be several reasons that the post doesn't show the expected reaction but mostly there is one big mistake: you shared the content based on your own preferences instead of what really matters to your audience. But hang on, didn't you find something that really suits them?

The trick is the hook line. The first three lines of a post with images and the first five line of a text-only post act as an opener. They include two magic words at the end: '...see more.' As we talked about earlier, clicking on that counts more for the algorithm than a like.

You have various options to create that hook line:

1. **Common question** with some details which can even be slightly provocative, e.g. "Who is that person beyond your ideal customer we all want to have in our network?"

2. **Value-based announcement** about the content including the most appealing fact within the hook, e.g. "Last year we increased our revenue by 30% just by doing this one thing."

3. **How-to list** providing clarity on how many points are following in the post, e.g. "How to be a Social Selling expert in seven simple steps."

4. **Challenge the status quo** by writing the opposite of a common opinion, e.g. "The lockdown period had a massive advantage which mankind would never have achieved otherwise."

5. **Personal story** revealing a secret or a special personal trick nobody knows, e.g. "I moved from Zürich to Sydney after a layoff. This is what I learned to restart my life."

Please be aware that the first 2.5 lines (or 4.5 lines if no image) are the only space you have available to get the reader interested in your post. If you are unsure, copy the text of any other post up to the 'see more' part to estimate the length you have available.

Not all professionals play the hook well. Some use a headline followed by a blank line like starting an article in traditional media. You can do the same on LinkedIn, but I see it as a waste of precious real estate. People who know your way of writing would be happy to see the latest episode of a series, but others would simply scroll on by as they miss the reason to read further.

These are my ideas to work on the hook so that it suits your network to get the desired reaction:

1. **Write** a magic intro showing exactly why that piece of content is relevant to your audience, what they can learn from it, how it helps in their shift from pain to gain. Add emojis like this one ✈.

2. **Choose** a suitable image for the post that acts as a scroll stopper. If it is based on a curated article, add the link to the original text after posting or in the first comment for a higher reach.

3. **Tag** up to five people in the post itself and the picture, then add up to ten others in the comments to entice a dialogue. Send the post link to those who are likely to react in a direct message.

4. **Share** the post at a time when your audience is in the right mood to see it. Use your favourite social media management platform to schedule for the right time to post (I recommend Hootsuite).

When you start crafting your open lines accordingly, a nice side effect will be visible not long afterwards: your writing will improve as you pay attention to the impact of your words.

☞ www.connectandactbook.com/hook

Appreciation

How can we disrupt the feed of our audience and surprise them? Sure, we can add even better content on the same topics as usual. We can publish the more impressive case study or an even more impactful customer win. Or we share even more interesting material from external sources to show we are experts by educating our tribe.

Impressive, impactful and interesting all start with the letter "I" but shouldn't we think about you? Instead of talking about ourselves why not occasionally some appreciation for the people in our network? Talking about that would be a welcome surprise for many!

Since coming to Australia only a couple of years ago, I've enjoyed building a strong network. It's important to learn from each other, given the different content areas and also to reach out when we need help. Being grateful for a well-composed group of people around us is important in any stage of business and personal life. Therefore LinkedIn for me is all about the depth of true connections instead of just a numbers game.

There are several ways to show genuine appreciation or gratefulness on LinkedIn. They all have in common that you show a message of thanks to someone for something. It can be visible to the public or happen privately.

Some years ago LinkedIn introduced their 'Kudos' format, a choice of set forms of recognition. You go to the profile you would like to recognise, click on 'More' and choose 'Give Kudos' with ten visual examples from 'Great Job' to 'Outside the Box Thinker' or 'Making an Impact'. You can choose whether this should appear as public post or in a direct message.

A less visible way is to endorse someone for their skills. It used to be more complicated as we had to choose the relationship we had by choosing their job title. It's an easy and often forgotten option. I see endorsements as a mix of acknowledging someone for their capabilities but also just to say hello in a "givers gain" approach.

Many people totally underestimate the power of saying "Thank you!" We all once learned that we should send a thank-you letter, email or LinkedIn message to a hiring manager within a job search process – but most candidates skip that step. A missed chance of just being polite.

Sending a personal thank-you note also sends a strong message to a person that we care about them. You can include emojis to underline your feelings if appropriate. What I *don't* recommend is using an impersonal note to several people at once or (even worse!) using an automation tool.

These are four simple steps to show appreciation to individuals or your whole network with quick activities:

1. **Write** a surprising shout-out about a colleague or to a business partner highlighting their contribution to your company, your personal growth or to your clients.

2. **Send** personal birthday wishes to those you know, like and trust, more than just the standard line when you see the reminder. Hint: sending that with a one-day delay will be more visible.

3. **Introduce** members of your network to each other, having their common interests in mind. You might be the reason for others to be successful – and this will surely come back in some form.

4. **Create** or curate material which celebrates personal growth or gratefulness to your network. This helps to lift the spirit of your audience and yourself when you read their comments.

You will surely recognise the positive energy generated from spreading goodwill to your network as a disrupting message in the sea of serious content and self-promotion. And you will surely welcome more positive people joining your audience, too!

☞ www.connectandactbook.com/appreciation

Newspaper

Ever thought about using LinkedIn in a slightly different way than most others do? Like a newspaper showing only relevant news to you, with yourself in the role of the editor?

Many professionals would like to be more active on LinkedIn but they perceive their feed as irrelevant and thus see no reason to engage. Soon they give up without addressing the source of the issue.

If you want to learn about a certain topic or be connected to experts in that space, LinkedIn is a great way to observe the trends, to find important players and get a fair range of opinions shared by others.

The time of seeing LinkedIn purely as an online CV is surely over as you have recognised in this book so far – despite the platform helping many to find their next opportunity.

But it is our own responsibility (and opportunity!) to enjoy a more relevant LinkedIn experience. Therefore I've mentioned on various occasions that we can treat it like a newspaper with a double role – we can read what we like and filter out most of the rest.

There are two areas users first look at on most social media channels:

1. The first group starts with the newsfeed, like zapping through the TV channels waiting for something interesting to appear.

2. The second group goes straight to the Notifications tab which is more relevant as the algorithm connects the dots for us.

I belong to the second group, knowing it's a better use of my time spent on social media.

But even the feed can be adopted towards our own preferences. Unfortunately, most users do not understand how. And the more they give a 'like' to something they actually don't want to see in the future, the more they will see something similar. That turns quickly into a negative spiral and adds further to their perception that using LinkedIn is useless.

It is in our own hands to tell the platform what we like which is easily possible by changing our behaviour. If we let LinkedIn know what we are interested in and mostly engage with the relevant content, then the algorithm will give us more of what we truly want to see. We just need to get started.

What is our benefit from this newspaper mindset? We can treat the action of being active on the various social media channels as a regular activity like in the good old days when we could not wait to get the newspaper delivered to our doorstep.

Remember reading the Sunday newspaper sitting in a nice armchair with a cup of tea, enjoying what you read? Or perhaps you might remember that from your parents!

These are my tips on how you can treat LinkedIn as a newspaper:

1. **Connect** with professionals of your industry, segment, territory, or other groups of interest. Disconnect from those people who do not engage with you (they can still follow you).

2. **Engage** yourself with topics of your area of interest or industry such as commenting on relevant posts, following companies or institutions in your space, and subscribing to relevant hashtags.

3. **Post** content serving your target audience to achieve an increased engagement rate, and as a result, more of the right content will come into your feed and increase your network.

4. **Start** your LinkedIn activities not in the feed but go directly to the notification tab instead; then your experience becomes much more relevant.

Welcome to your new role as editor, serving precisely one very important reader – you!

☞ www.connectandactbook.com/newspaper

Converting Well in Practice

Here are some further ideas from experts in my network.

Michael Haynes

SME Business Growth Specialist, Founder of the Legacy SME B2B Community, author of "Listen Innovate Grow" (Sydney)
www.linkedin.com/in/michaelhhaynes

Social Selling is relevant and applicable in the everchanging world of B2B. However, there are three fundamentals that should be adhered to, to help ensure your success.

Your number one objective during all your interactions with B2B customers and prospects is to provide A-I-R (Advice, Insights and Recommendations) to help them achieve their objectives. B2B buyers want to identify new opportunities and ways of doing things, make sense of all the different ideas and perspectives ("noise") they are continually bombarded with and learn how to create solution alternatives and make trade-offs.

Think broadly in terms of the different formats that you can use to engage and interact with B2B buyers. For instance, livestream discussions which can be done via platforms such as LinkedIn and Streamyard are a great way to provide insights and demonstrate expertise, as well as provide an opportunity for buyers to ask questions and share ideas.

Distribute your content broadly. Be where your buyers are! Platforms that are particularly effective in reaching B2B buyers include LinkedIn, YouTube, Medium and online communities and forums.

Larry Levine

*Catalyst for Sales Culture Change, podcaster and author of
"Selling From The Heart" (Los Angeles)*
www.linkedin.com/in/larrylevine1992

Brian Tracy once said, "Lack of clarity is the primary reason for failure in business and personal life."

Clarity – this becomes even more important as we bring social media into the equation. Social platforms have become the hot spot for distortions, filters and where the real versions of who we are remain backstage.

We take selfies. We photoshop, curate and upload the best we've got, then we hold our breath and pray for attention. In the world of social media, social acting, fantasy and a filtered lifestyle has become the norm.

Let's think like one of your clients or a future client for a moment... do you ever wonder if this thought runs through their mind? *Stop trying to impress me. I can make up my own mind about whether I like you, trust you or even believe you. You don't have to make up my mind for me.*

When you bring clarity to the forefront, when you bring conciseness to the forefront and when you bring conviction to the forefront, you enable people to make better decisions which create better outcomes.

Whether this be face-to-face interactions or how you choose to interact online, in today's business environment this of the utmost importance.

People are watching you! Clarity avoids misunderstandings. Clarity builds trust. Clarity leaves a lasting impression.

Monika Ruzicka Kenter

Global Business Development & Customer Success Manager at ReadyForSocial by Thought Horizon (Atlanta)

www.linkedin.com/in/monikaruzicka

In my opinion, listening to your target audience on LinkedIn is one of the key ingredients to conversion.

I connect with and follow decision-makers and influencers or track them via LinkedIn Sales Navigator. Then, I closely monitor the content they share, learn about them and look for hooks that I can turn into micro-conversions, something that moves my relationship towards a deal.

I really try to understand where they are in their journey and what value I can offer – from an insightful tip in the form of a comment, to a piece of content or a conversation – until they are ready for more.

Andreas Jonsson

Founder & CEO at Shield – LinkedIn analytics for teams and individuals @ shieldapp.ai (Copenhagen)

www.linkedin.com/in/ajonxyz

Posting original content is the backbone of your LinkedIn profile. And when you want to win on LinkedIn, you gotta learn what works. Without your data, you're not seeing the full picture.

The biggest influencers and the best sellers rely on data to generate unique insights based on their performance. With data at your fingertips, you can learn what works much faster.

Attract the right audience, start the right conversations, build win-win relationships. Don't sell yourself short. Publish consistently, dive into the data, and start winning instead.

Summary

You made it through all chapters! I'm sure that now you understand what I meant with *systematic* in the subtitle of this book. Now you have all the vital instruments in your hands to become a successful social seller!

Here are four key takeaways from this chapter:

The target of Social Selling is advancing business conversations. Therefore it is not enough to build a network based on a genuine personal brand by posting content regularly, you also need to convert the conversations to the final step depending on their position in the funnel.

Timing is a critical factor which starts with planning your activities and goes further to how we nurture and follow up the started conversations. The key here is using a multi-channel approach with a well-prepared cadence instead of relying on LinkedIn as the only platform.

Direct messaging is one of the key functions within LinkedIn if you know how to operate it well. You can add voice and video to your messages and filter the inbox to avoid losing your conversations. You can even create your own chat groups for your inner circle.

From understanding metrics to using advanced tools such as the Sales Navigator edition, LinkedIn offers a range of tools to support conversion activities. Whatever you do to be successful, it starts with your mindset. In my view, LinkedIn is a newspaper and you are the editor!

Finish

Conclusion

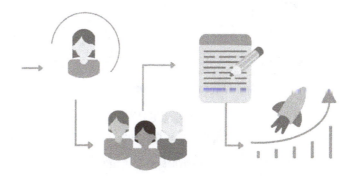

"A conclusion is simply the place where you got tired of thinking."

Dan Chaon

Action

Most people scroll through their feed on LinkedIn and wonder why the content is not relevant to them. But around two percent of all members change that by making LinkedIn all their own.

We will never be able to enjoy our journey on the platform in the long term if we allow the experience to be dictated by the system.

It is up to all of us to influence our feed with 👇

- the professionals you engage with
- the newsletters you subscribe to
- the hashtags you follow
- the content you like

Instead of scrolling the feed and wasting your precious time, I recommend going directly to your notifications tab to see what matters, including:

- congratulations as invitations to engage
- notifications from your audience
- reactions on your content
- news of relevance

It's not difficult to:

- add your view
- share your thoughts
- explain why it resonates
- give further examples to the post
- be provocative by challenging others

Here's what you can do to achieve this:

1. **Comment** on the posts of those people who share great content in a similar niche, geography, industry, or who have some other things in common. Choose those who also have a decent following.

2. **Connect** with like-minded professionals from those areas who are regularly commenting on others – they might pay back the favour on your own content.

3. **Contact** them to learn more about what they do. Don't pitch to them straight away; instead, build relationships as they might become your cheerleaders along the journey.

4. **Collaborate** with their network based on your comments and content. This is where the gold mine is located. It is in your hands to have a fantastic experience, creating the desire to come back.

When you start using Social Selling strategies for yourself you'll be surprised how many more relevant professionals you'll welcome into your network. Plus your feed won't be crowded with irrelevant stuff anymore.

Give it a try by changing your behaviour and start regularly commenting on the posts of others. I am keen to learn from you and happily return the favour by engaging with your content as well.

P.S. Did you recognise the unusual visual appearance of the last page? The first two bullet point lists nail down their elements to the point. The third one instead builds itself from short to long for an optical demonstration of the growth by applying activities.

Successful content creators such as Justin Welsh and Ryan Musselman use this method on purpose to convey their message in an optical way as well. You can find useful examples in the link below.

☞ www.connectandactbook.com/action

Enjoy

Congratulations, you made it! Thank you so much for reading my book and learning more about the different aspects of Social Selling and how they are interconnected.

I'm sure you already noticed early on how the various topics raised in this book across the double page layout can relate to you. Here are my tips as to how you can make the best out of what you've read so far (or if you've skipped straight to the end as some people like to do for a preview):

1. **Action**: You can put in practice what you learned, one step at a time. Simply follow the flow as outlined in the book, remembering the LEGO® bricks story I mentioned at the beginning.

2. **Reference**: Alternatively or in addition to the first step you can use this book rather as a guide to go back to, ad-hoc or regularly, to apply changes to your LinkedIn activities.

You might have recognised that the book can also be adopted a bit further beyond LinkedIn as many of the principles work on other channels as well. You might want to fix your LinkedIn activities first and then adapt your Facebook, Instagram and Twitter profiles afterwards.

Initially I wanted to call the book *Collect or Connect?* to point to the difference between a pointless collection of names on a list and genuine connections. It was ultimately titled, *Connect & Act* as any connection makes no sense without action. No content will move a needle without converting. And your personal brand won't connect without you acting on the refresh beforehand.

The subtitle covers *Systematic Social Selling*. Coming from Switzerland with German origins, I love a system approach to see patterns instead of just following an order of tasks. Therefore I carefully used this structure of double pages which you can easily put into action.

Below on the cover you can read the sentence, *A practical guidebook to using LinkedIn for your profile, pleasure and profit.* We talked about the practical aspect of the double pages book already. Why do you think there are exactly 42 of them?

Did you also realise that every double page is named with just one word? This is to highlight the importance of simplicity. Improving LinkedIn doesn't have to be complicated. Take a simple and easy approach; your readers will thank you for that.

The words with "P" underline the outcome. Obviously you will improve your LinkedIn profile after applying what you learned in the book. If you work in a sales-related role running prospecting and selling activities, then you will see that pleasure and profit will be the result.

But why pleasure in this context? Rarely have I heard someone talking about the nice time you can have while being on LinkedIn! Treat it like your own newspaper as I mentioned earlier. In the good old days, people enjoyed reading well-written articles about entertaining topics in addition to the ordinary news, while seated in a comfortable chair with a good cup of tea.

It is the same with LinkedIn. Please think about reading elegantly formulated articles on topics like personal development, the latest trends in your profession or anything you like to deep dive in. This can be a pleasure!

If you would like to receive the PDF of this book, please use the keyword *pleasure* in the form on www.connectandactbook.com/pdf.

Enjoy your Social Selling activities and let me know if I can help you in any way – I am just a (personalised) connection or an email away!

CONTENT CREATOR

One More Thing

Cabinet

"The only source of knowledge is experience."

Albert Einstein

Workbooks

This book comes with three practical aspects: on one hand it works as a reference for a later stage if you want to go back to a particular section and put your learning into practice.

The second level is the link selection below each double page with further reading such as examples and additional background. This is my contribution to keep the content updated for my readers.

The third element is the set of workbooks from my coaching programs. Of course they might work differently per industry or market. The way we invite someone to our network in English is more casual than in German where we would more formally address a stranger by their last name.

From my experience of those programs I developed a transferrable set of documents which I include behind the link below:

1. **Complete**: Profile checklists with different versions for employees in companies and for entrepreneurs.

2. **Connect**: Templates to invite other people to your network and respond to invitations, which you can adopt for your usage.

3. **Content**: A growing selection of post templates derived from global creators for many occasions plus content strategy examples.

4. **Convert**: Workbooks for time management and converting direct messages along the funnel journey.

I am keen to learn how those workbooks and templates help you to be successful on your Social Selling journey. Please feel free to add comments and suggestions on how to improve them.

☞ www.connectandactbook.com/workbooks

Online Course

There are three ways to learn a complex topic such as Social Selling: you can read a book like this one *and* put it into action. You can attend a group or individual coaching program with accountability to apply what you learned. Or you can attend a recorded online course at your own pace *and* act upon what the facilitator taught you.

I created my second online course around the same four chapters as this book which later turned to the concept of those LEGO® bricks. It also comes with a range of workbooks and further reading to prepare my students in the best possible way to learn by promoting running their own activities.

For this book I have expanded the course further to align with what my students and I learned in the meantime.

The online course with more than 90 mins of recorded lessons is the ideal companion to this book. As you have already bought my book, I am happy to welcome you as a new student for 20% off the regular price.

☞ www.connectandactbook.com/courseforreaders

Recommended Reading

Lifelong learning: without a range of books and followed content creators my Social Selling journey would be impossible. My passion about this topic led to the earlier events in my Meetup group, my online courses, the regular webinars, my employment at Hootsuite and this book. Thanks to LinkedIn and living in Sydney, I've had the chance to meet many of them in person. Time to recognise some of the authors and their work here.

Richard Bliss: **Digital-First Leadership**, 2021. Knowing Richard from our mutual time in the software industry, I admire his content towards social media for top leaders and enjoyed being an early guest in his podcast.

Damian Corbet: **The Social CEO: How Social Media Can Make You a Stronger Leader**, 2019. Damian's action-provoking book shows senior leaders how to embrace and master the social age to survive.

Wendy Lloyd Curley: **Stop Wasting Your Time Networking**, 2021. This book is the ultimate guide about networking both offline and online to market businesses through personal connections.

Daniel Disney, **The Ultimate LinkedIn Sales Guide**, 2021. I followed his sales blog and online course for years before he became an author; for me this book is one of the best Social Selling references out there.

Michele Gennoe: **Mindful Leadership**, 2020. This book shows seven practical steps how to achieve mindful leadership as a timeless inspiration and how leaders can become more mindful in leading themselves and others.

Michael Haynes and Garreth Chandler: **Listen Innovate Grow**, 2018. Remarkable guidebook for start-ups and SMEs to acquire and grow business to business customers, highly practical with adaptable case studies.

Ryan Holmes: **Saving Social: The Dysfunctional Past and Promising Future of Social Media**, 2021. Ryan founded Hootsuite as the first social media management platform; no wonder his insights are respected globally.

Tony J. Hughes: **The Joshua Principle: Leadership Secrets of Selling**, 2013. One of the most influential sales book authors in APAC describes a new sales methodology in a wonderful story about sales mentorship.

Jane Jackson: **Navigating Career Crossroads**, 2020. Changing careers requires courage and a trustworthy guide like Jane's book. For me, one of the most useful reference books, alongside her coaching and podcast episodes.

Mark McInnes: **Tactical Pipeline Growth**, 2020. Highly practical sales book to win the outbound battle for new business from one of Australia's best Social Sellers, full of speed and tactical guidance to implement ASAP.

Cian McLoughlin: **Rebirth of the Salesman**, 2015. One of my favourite sales books of all time, Cian researched the background for wins and losses. My book review series started by writing about this important publication.

Jamie Shanks: **Social Selling Mastery**, 2016. Early foundational work about Social Selling for corporate sales professionals which I finished while attending the online course of his company, Sales for Life.

John Smibert, Wayne Moloney, Jeff Clulow: **The Wentworth Prospect**, 2021. One of the best enterprise sales novels I've ever read, including Social Selling as one of the principles used by the fictitious protagonist.

Shani Taylor: **From Ignored to Adored**, 2022. This book transforms the feeling of ignorance in endless social media feeds into building true human connections with your soul-mate clients without being salesy.

Brynne Tillman: **The LinkedIn Sales Playbook: A Tactical Guide to Social Selling**, 2017. Impressive combination of book and pre-recorded webinars for readers covering only highly practical tips for sales professionals.

Please follow my bi-weekly LinkedIn newsletter **"Learn From Books"** covering detailed reviews about books in the areas of sales, leadership and entrepreneurship, including insightful interviews with the authors.

☞ www.connectandactbook.com/newsletter

Quick Links

Here is a list of easy ways to access functions within LinkedIn in a faster way than going through all the menu options. This is especially handy when you quickly want to do something and can't find the way to solve it easily. Or perhaps you want to go back to a certain place regularly, e.g. checking your followers or researching hashtags for your content.

Many links can be typed into the browser directly, for others you need to replace <username> with the name shown in your profile URL. You can find updates to this list using the link at the bottom of the page.

- Posts: www.linkedin.com/in/<username>/detail/recent-activity/shares
- Articles: www.linkedin.com/in/<username>/detail/recent-activity/posts
- Saved posts: www.linkedin.com/my-items/saved-posts
- Followed members: www.linkedin.com/feed/following
- Your followers: www.linkedin.com/feed/followers
- Follower not member: www.linkedin.com/feed/following/?filterType=member
- Who viewed your profile: www.linkedin.com/me/profile-views
- Received invites: www.linkedin.com/mynetwork/invitation-manager
- Sent invites: www.linkedin.com/mynetwork/invitation-manager/sent
- Recommendation: www.linkedin.com/in/<username>/detail/recommendation/write
- Discover hub: www.linkedin.com/mynetwork/discover-hub
- Newsletters: www.linkedin.com/mynetwork/network-manager/newsletters
- Followed pages: www.linkedin.com/mynetwork/network-manager/company
- Followed hashtags: www.linkedin.com/mynetwork/network-manager/hashtags
- Concrete hashtag: www.linkedin.com/feed/hashtag/<hashtag>
- Your groups: www.linkedin.com/groups
- Social Selling Index: www.linkedin.com/sales/ssi

☞ www.connectandactbook.com/quicklinks

About the Author

Gunnar moved to Australia in 2016 after a layoff from his corporate career in Switzerland which has spanned Consulting over Product Marketing and Business Development to Sales Management, covering the local market and later overseeing a European region covering 29 countries.

A born introvert, it took him a while to even consider becoming visible. Moving across four countries, he found LinkedIn to be the best way to create a personal brand and build meaningful connections. As a strategic networker and Social Selling advocate, he believes in the power of social media activities to champion the power of human connections.

Passionate about the transformation of modern workplaces to embrace new ways of collaboration, Gunnar blogs about social media, leadership, networking and sales excellence. He obtained an Advanced Diploma of Leadership and Management at the Australian Institute of Management (AIM) in Sydney and received the Chartered Manager designation from the Institute of Managers and Leaders (IML) where he is mentoring the next generation of leaders. Before that, he completed his Master of Computer Science in Germany and Advanced Studies in Business Administration in his hometown of Zürich in Switzerland.

His Australian work experience began at KeepItSafe, a Managed Service Provider in the Business Continuity discipline, before adding a consulting channel to the Risk Management software vendor Noggin.

Being recognised for his Social Selling activities outside of his corporate role, he joined Hootsuite as Senior Partner & Alliance Manager for APAC where he improved their industry-standard Social Selling course by adding the missing practical side.

In his following role as Senior Partner Manager at GoTo, he built a partner business for IT Management solutions to help resellers and Managed Service Providers making IT easy, anywhere.

His regular LinkedIn Power Lab webinars include free hands-on tips around various aspects from content to conversion, helping business owners and executives transition their approach from "collect to connect" to build meaningful, mutually fruitful relationships.

Gunnar has been featured in several podcasts and interviews highlighting the importance of relationships with a 'givers gain' approach. For the Institute of Managers and Leaders he has delivered Masterclasses about the transition from an accidental manager to an intentional leader. He has published 24 books so far, most of them about travel and tourism in German.

His Australian book contributions were published in *Lessons I Learnt* about turning his own corporate layoff situation into a sustainable advantage, *Leaders of Influence* about the transition from an accidental manager to an intentional leader and *Leading Well* with a case study about curiosity being at the heart of emotional intelligence.

Connecting all his experiences together, he enjoys learning the governance level as a Board Director firsthand in the historic Castlereagh Boutique Hotel in Sydney following his vision that social media should have a seat at the board table.

Connect with the author here:

☞ www.gunnarhabitz.com.au, gunnar@gunnarhabitz.com.au

☞ www.linkedin.com/in/gunnarhabitz